THE CUSTOMERS ALWAYS WRITE

...the untold stories!

C. DEANDRE' SMITH

Copyright © 2025 **Charles DeAndre Smith**

All rights reserved. No part of this publication may be reproduced, distributed, or transmitted in any form or by any means, including photocopying, recording, or other electronic or mechanical methods, without the prior written permission of the publisher, except in the case of brief quotations embodied in critical reviews and certain other noncommercial uses permitted by copyright law. For permission requests, write to the publisher, addressed "Attention: Book Rights and Permission," at the address below.

Published in the United States of America

ISBN 978-1-956741-62-9 (SC)
ISBN 978-1-961507-64-7 (HC)
ISBN 978-1-961507-65-4 (Ebook)

Library of Congress Control Number: 2024926764

Charles DeAndre Smith
978 Angelus Ave
San Diego, CA 92114
www.stellarliterary.com

Order Information and Rights Permission:

Quantity sales. Special discounts might be available on quantity purchases by corporations, associations, and others. For details, contact the publisher at the address above.

For Book Rights Adaptation and other Rights Permission.
Call us at toll-free 1-888-945-8513 or send us an email at
admin@stellarliterary.com.

Dedicated to three people who define the word family:
Charles E. Smith, Christine E. Smith, and Phyllis Adrienne Smith.

CONTENTS

LA EX	1
VIDEO EXPO	5
GIMME AN O	13
WHEN A STRANGER CALLS	17
WHERE EVERYBODY KNOWS YOUR NAME	21
DIFFERENT FOLKS, SAME STROKES	28
WHO YOU GONNA CALL?	35
STRAYS	42
BIRDS OF A FEATHER	47
RAP, ROCK, RESPECT	56
WALKING THE DOG	69
BEHIND CLOSED DOORS	77
THINK TANK	85
"SPILL IN BOOTH 2!"	93
BOYS WILL BE ... GIRLS	99
OH MAN(NEQUIN)!	112
OTTERS AND COUGARS AND BEARS— OH MY!	118
SLIP-SLIDIN' AWAY	127
JURASSIC PORN	139
50 SHADES OF DRÉ	146
JEWISH GUILT	155
TALE OF THE TAPE	166
LESBIFRIENDS	173
SUCKER FOR LOVE	187
THE CASE OF THE MISSING DIARY	199
CAUGHT IN THE MATRIX	209
SINCE MY LAST CONFESSION	225
HALL OF FAME/WALL OF SHAME	240
RETURN FLIGHT	258

LA EX

This was a breakup of the catastrophic kind. It was acrimonious at best. No well wishes. No cordial parting of the ways. No amicable split. No. This was a see-you-never-again-here-is-my-back-have-a- fucked-up-life type of separation, so I had to get as far away from Los Angeles as possible—south anyway. I was in search of a new love. Destination: San Diego, a city known for its beautiful, sunny weather, described as the best climate on earth. A world-famous zoo, host to Comic-Con (the most renowned yearly comic convention in the United States and one of the largest business gatherings in the world). A veritable tourist haven.

These were glowing credentials indeed. She sounded so intriguing. So inviting. So perfect. But so what? I had yet to escape LA's city limits and I missed her already: the smog-filled skies, the debris-littered streets, the pockets of congestion caused by impatient drivers packed inside overpriced vehicles like sardines on overly populated roads.

Stop it, André!

There I was, bounding down the 405 freeway, barely outside of LA County, and I was al-ready waxing nostalgic over my City of Angels. Bah! Not an apt description. City of *Fallen* Angels, perhaps! Where she-devils run amok and will trample you from all four directions.

The metropolis spawns them, trains them, teaches them how to take advantage of man's true weakness: his ego. I've always heard it said that women are smarter than men. (I'm sure that's a rumor started by a woman—who was right!) Yes, men lie. So do women. The difference being that women are much better at it!

They take our Achilles' heel, dress it up in some designer shoe, and walk us down the road to ruin—at least that was my beaten path. So it comes as no surprise that there were more tremors felt than stable ground enjoyed in my personal relationships. Sure, in between my first love (a pampered princess) and my worst nightmare (a psychotic, pathological liar), I had some meaningful encounters ... but nothing lasting. And the latter association proved to be my proverbial last straw, breaking my will, spirit, and—nearly—bank account.

My failed professional life was also playing a part in my hasty departure. The clichéd promise of fame and fortune had awaited me at one time in the form of a freelance writing job at the *Los Angeles Times*. The *LA Times*! Hired straight out of college, twenty-one years old, green as a Douglas fir. The LA Times! It wasn't a full-time gig, but at least I could sleep over at the big, beautiful journalistic mansion; besides, it would be only a matter of time before I got my own room, right? The LA Times!

Fast-forward three years, and my byline still read, "Special To The Times." No staff writer position. No employee benefits. No shelter from the upcoming storm. Drastic budget cuts were on the horizon, massive job loss. But I was told not to worry because the section I wrote for, the *City Times*, was "untouchable."

Untouchable. Elliot Ness learned the hard way that the word itself is a veritable contradiction—as did I. *The City Times* proved to be more fatted calf than sacred cow, as it was led off to slaughter along with many other departments. The editor of the *LA Times* courted me for weeks, giving me the impression that I wouldn't be among the unemployed. I figured that even though my ship was sinking, surely a life boat would be thrown my way via a promotion—but in the eleventh hour, I received no stay of execution. This ushered in the beginning of my journalistic end. My foundation was rocked, my heart broken.

With so much old baggage, a new start seemed to be a certified no-brainer, so off I sped. Glancing out the passenger window at the gorgeous Pacific horizon, I couldn't tell where the sapphire-blue waters ended and the cloudless sky began. I didn't care, either. For a highly analytical mind like mine, finding refuge in the unknown was a welcome rarity.

Little did I know as I cruised down the California coast that I was embarking on the next leg of my journey, on a collision course with a story far bigger than any other I had covered. The storm clouds that had washed away a once promising career carried with them a silver lining that my tired, weepy eyes could not yet see.

In time, I would learn that my ex had actually done me a favor, kicking me out of the nest. Wings now broken would eventually heal, become fully functional again, and allow a once-wounded bird to soar to new heights of enlightenment. Confusion would give way to clarity, animosity to acceptance, prejudices to keen perception. Although I had once seen myself as innocent victim, I would come to the realization that at times, I too played the part of guilty culprit.

This process would take well over eight years to unfold—double the time of my under-graduate work at Loyola Marymount University. As a journalist, I had been taught to keep a safe emotional distance from my subjects, thus allowing for greater objectivity; personal feelings can only serve to taint the finished product. That's how it should work but is not how it always turns out.

Sometimes, a story is so powerful that it not only captivates the reader but also influences the writer. I would discover that the people you never expect to make the slightest mark on your consciousness are the very ones that leave an indelible impression.

My subjects were waiting, life-changing conversations at the ready, interviews to be conducted in the most unlikely of venues.

VIDEO EXPO

Well, there I was in San Diego.

Languishing away in the hot California sun for the past four hours, handing out job resumes had me at wit's end, and all I had to show for my efforts were a parched throat, a sweat-soaked shirt, and sore feet.

The list of possible employers was long and undistinguished—a few convenience stores, the local library, a gas station; but beggars indeed cannot be choosers.

I needed to find something soon, because what little money I had saved was quickly running out—and rent was due. I was unemployed for three months before I left LA, so I could not afford to spend my second month in San Diego jobless. Time being of the essence meant I had to make each minute count, but I feared that a second longer in this July heat would be my undoing. As the indomitable Vince Lombardi once proclaimed; "Fatigue makes cowards of us all."

Before I sought out the refuge of my nearby air-conditioned (albeit claustrophobic) one-bed-room apartment, however, I needed to run one last errand: return an item. Completion of he task wouldn't require any additional walking, as I had to travel in the same direction to reach my car. This endeavor would also provide temporary shelter from the noonday sun.

As I approached my destination, I found myself being overtaken by a bout of paranoia. Even though no one was around, it still felt like someone or *something* was watching me, mocking. Laughing. Oddly enough, I had been here just last night and hadn't experienced this feeling. Something was different this time, though.

It turns out, this visit would mark another major shift in my universe, would be the next seminal moment in my life. For the second time in less than eighteen hours, I found myself standing in front of this dark-tinted door, the difference now being that my head was swiveling from side to side, shooting quick glances over each shoulder. I cautiously reached out and pushed the handle forward, re- immersing myself into the alternate reality that is a pornography shop.

The highly volatile marriage of X-rated sights and guttural moans would have been enough to push one of a weaker sexual constitution into sensory overload—a dilemma I would soon witness others experiencing—but I remained steady, true to my purpose. My over-whelming desire to be face to face with the television (remote in one hand, Corona in the other) resulted in my beeline toward the counter—and an inevitable date with destiny.

I grabbed the DVD out of my briefcase and placed it on the counter in front of the clerk, not realizing I was handing over the key to Pandora's box, oblivious to the forces I was about to unleash. Making eye contact, I informed the guy behind the counter, "I am returning this rental." He was young. A boy, really. My junior by approximately fifteen years. Baby-faced, he had cornrows braided in a zigzagging pattern across his scalp. He was a stark contrast to the bearded old man the night before, who had looked like Old Mac- Donald and, well, had a smell that made me think, *E-I-E-I-O!*

Apparently, this nineties kid took me to be in a joking mood and decided to serve up a bit of remedial humor. "Great flick, huh?"

I decided to reply. If nothing else, the dialogue would keep me indoors for a little while longer—not to mention, I have never been one to back away from an opportunity to engage in witty repartee— as witty as this could get. "None of the actors have a gold statue in their immediate future," I responded, "but mission accomplished."

The raising of his right brow was verification that I had wasted a perfectly inserted Oscar reference; however, he obviously understood the latter part of my statement, as evidenced by his forthcoming sinful smile. "It's our red-hot flick of the month," he blurted out while handing back my $40 deposit. I suppose I could see why the movie would garner some interest with a title like *The Road to Suckcess!* Hell, it had made me curious.

I was starting to feel better. Central air works wonders on a hot, muggy day. Because of this fact, my playful ribbing continued. "Mighty tough gig being surrounded by tits and clits all day, huh?"

"No, no, not at all, man!" he countered, clearly misreading my sarcasm. "This is the easiest job in the fuckin' world, bro! I read porn. I watch porn. I sell porn all day. What more could a guy ask for?!"

Yeah, he was about nineteen, all right. But that didn't make his answer any less valid. As they say, "From the mouth of babes …" I mean, what daily challenges could he possibly face on this job? How to dress the mannequin? Deciding whether to put *How Harry Ate Sally* in the "parodies" or "new releases" section?

Considering the two employees I had encountered, the screening process couldn't be very rigorous—if one even existed—and I needed to find work! At that moment, the punchline revealed itself to me and I realized I was the butt of the joke! I envisioned the headline: "Aspiring journalist starts out on top—and ends up peddling well- oiled bottoms." That was the mockery! I envisioned my ex laughing hysterically, cracking herself up. (Yeah, she was a real bitch, but I still loved her.)

You see, while working in LA as a writer, I had lived in the San Fernando Valley, an area so well known for its prolific adult-film production that it has been dubbed, appropriately enough, Porn Valley. Now I had moved more than two hours away just to consider making a living selling all things pornographic? Irony, thy name is life!

I did a life comparison. Then: a college degree, the *LA Times*, recognition, self-fulfillment, the beginnings of greatness. Now: a no-degree-necessary job at a porn shop, judgments, stereotypes, corporate ceiling right above my head.

I paused for a second and recalled a scene from the movie Rambo: The betrayed hero, resolute in his conviction, is being interrogated—basically tortured—by enemy soldiers attempting to extract information. Their rancorous leader looks on, taking pleasure in his prisoner's pain. "Pride is a poor substitute for intelligence," he taunts.

The wise words snap me back to reality: Bills. Rent. Car. Gas and electric. Food. Fuck my ex! "Hey, young man! Let me get an application."

THE MANTRA

"Oh, don't worry about that couple outside," Jacques, the night janitor, reassured me. "It's their Friday-night foreplay." He continued to diligently mop the floor.

"They go to the bar, get drunk, argue, come in and buy a toy, then leave the happy couple. Don't be shocked."

Shocked?! Oh, I thought, this wasn't shocking. Shock had been when a week had passed and I hadn't heard back from Video Expo after submitting my application. Seriously, if I couldn't get a job at a porn shop, my only other prospect was spinning signs on the corner for a fast-food chain or income tax company. At thirty-five.

Fortunately, I had escaped that most embarrassing possibility when I had finally received a phone call inquiring about my work availability. In time, I would learn that the reason for the delay had been that with my credentials, I appeared overqualified and management felt I would leave as soon as a better opportunity came along, as most clerks do.

Shock was when I had to restock an A-frame with all gay videos for the first time. It had taken about a month before I could even enter that section of the store without some sort of visceral reaction. But you can't blame me for that response—the homosexual acts that my heterosexual eyes had borne witness to for the first time would be enough to emotionally scar any straight man. Further adding to my anxiety had been a three-foot-long in-flatable penis (complete with testicles) that hung like a zeppelin from the ceiling above the gay section.

Shock was living near West Hollywood (better known as "West- Ho") and having kisses blown at me by a middle-aged Vietnamese queen in a sky-blue Thunderbird. Shock was being visually undressed and devoured by a pair of hungry eyes belonging to a half-Black, half-Hispanic waiter sporting a five-o-clock shadow while waiting to receive a to-go order of Oreo Cheesecake at the Cheesecake Factory.

And then there is *shock and awe!*

Like the time I was having lunch with Katrina at a popular eatery in Pasadena called Q's Billiards. She was a former high-school volleyball player who was paying her way through college as a part-time exotic dancer. (Of course, I am all for contributing to the cause of those in pursuit of higher learning.) Suddenly, I had noticed a slender, well-dressed man approaching us at the bar. I had assumed he was coming to see the bartender. I couldn't have been more wrong!

Subtlety be damned. "Can I buy you a drink?" he had offered. The nerve of this guy! But that is LA. In New York City, they try to steal the clothes right off your back; here, they try to steal the girl right from under your nose.

Kat—as I affectionately called her—could sense the rise in my testosterone level and decided to quickly intervene. "No thank you," she politely declined. Firm, straightforward, and done with a hint of appreciation for a kind gesture. Yet none of that mattered to him. He didn't acknowledge any of those things. He didn't budge. The nerve of this guy!

Before I could speak, I was once again beaten to the punch—this time not by the beautiful stripper but the beautiful stranger. "No, sweetheart, I was actually talking to him!"

It felt like we were experiencing an earthquake! The floor seemed to shake, and my legs felt weak. The city was experiencing mild tremors, perhaps? That's when I looked around and realized I was the only one wobbling on steady ground. Several seconds—that seemed like minutes—passed before I could articulate a response.

I eventually managed to gather my wits about me despite Kat's chuckles in my right ear.

A long, drawn-out breath precluded my somewhat mystified gaze back into my suitor's hazel eyes. Still in disbelief (and partial denial), I followed Kat's lead and repeated, "No thank you."

After these experiences, I was beginning to think nothing could shock, surprise, or even startle me at this point ... very foolish!

The couple's voices outside became more audible and distinct as they approached the store. The two were engaged in a definite dispute, but it appeared to be more passionate discussion than heated debate—or so I thought.

The lady barreled through the door, highly annoyed, with jealous boyfriend in tow. "You need to stop being like this!" she griped. "You know I like to come in here. You know why! And you need to get over it. I can't believe you're getting insecure over a vibrator! It's not a real person, and it's not like I am cheating on you!"

Her argument didn't sway him in the least as he continued to paw at her like a kid trying to get his mother's attention. He didn't want her to have any part of the orgasm-inducing gadgets hanging from the wall. After realizing his attempts to dissuade her were futile, however, the little boy stormed out the store.

That was a first for me because, although it's common to see a kid get angry because he can't have a toy, it is unusual behavior to see a kid get angry because Mommy is getting a toy. Actually, Mommy walked up to the counter with two toys: a Light-Me-Up Bullet and Waterproof Power Stud—a modern-day threesome for the sexually deprived woman. Reeking of alcohol, she belched, "I'll take these!"

Per store procedure, I put batteries in both items to ensure the merchandise was not faulty. This serves a dual purpose. First, there is nothing more upsetting to a horny woman than getting home and realizing that the flashy, seven-function vibrator she just spent money on is broken, and second, there is nothing more annoying to a clerk than arguing with a horny woman who is trying to return a vibrator that she says never worked … but she has obviously used. (Yes, it happens.)

Thankfully, both toys passed the customer's watchful inspection. Every wiggle and gyration was met with a lustful smile. "Yes!" she shrieked. "Those will do just fine."

Curiosity finally got the best of me. "What was your companion's problem?" I inquired.

"He said I don't need toys and that I am wasting money," she answered. "I waitress next door and make my own money, so I can spend it how I like—and if he completely satisfied me, I wouldn't want the toys!" Well, that explained his issue. But she then retracted her statement. "That isn't true. … I would get the toys regardless. I love them!"

What she followed with next would go down as arguably the most memorable quote in Video Expo history. I suppose it was only fitting that, in an ocean full of obscenities, a pearl of wisdom would be dropped from the rotten-toothed mouth of a crystal-methadone addict. Words that succinctly define adult behavior from the female perspective. (Go figure!) Waxing profound, she stated, "God gave it to me, and I am going to play with it!"

Shocked again.

GIMME AN O

Because there was no DVR back in the days when I first started working for Video Expo, I missed all the prime-time shows between three and eleven p.m.—not just the sitcoms on the local stations or the adult dramas on the pay channels, but also the sporting events and documentaries I always enjoyed. If whatever I was watching didn't end by 2:30, I was out of luck!

Fortunately for me, one Monday (a day off), I came across an intriguing special broadcast on the history of vibrators. Six months prior, I would have surfed right by this channel, but because I was in the profession of adult pleasures, I felt it would behoove me to tune in to the ninety-minute history lesson about the toy of the adult novelty business.

Apparently, these mini money-makers—it is estimated that one-third of adult American women own at least one—were initially designed to help cure "hysteria" back in the nineteenth century.[1] Anxiety, sleeplessness, irritability and nervousness were among the reported symptoms of this supposed female ailment. It turns out, these women were suffering from sexual frustration. Simply put—they were horny!

The prevailing thought at the time, however, was that women didn't have sex drives. American and European men—physicians included—believed that women did not experience sexual desire or pleasure, so doctors remained in the dark despite reported symptoms of erotic

---

[1] "'Hysteria' and the Strange History of Vibrators," Psychology Today, Michael Castleman, MA: https://www.psy-chologytoday.com/blog/all-about-sex/201303/hysteria-and-the-strange-history-vibrators

fantasies, feelings of heaviness in the lower abdomen, and wetness between the legs.

(Perhaps these were the forefathers of that sect of mankind that women describe as being clueless in the bedroom!)

The prescribed treatment for hysteria was genital massage, which doctors would administer in their offices. It proved to be successful, as well as wildly popular and profitable. (This problem-solving technique gives new meaning to the saying, "Take two (fingers) and call me in the morning.")

Although this remedy proved pleasurable for women, it became a painful procedure for the male practitioners. Doctors began to suffer from sore hands and achy fingers. Eventually, mechanical substitutes were invented, and in time, the vibrator was born. Business boomed, and the vibrator soon became one of the most purchased novelty items among women, just as it is today.

Per this documentary, three-quarters of the female population need direct clitoral stimulation because most intercourse doesn't supply much—a statistic supported by one of my past relationships with a tall blue-eyed brunette named Mallory. Before we dated, she informed me that she had experienced only a handful of internal orgasms in six years of sexual activity with over a dozen sexual partners. Her reason for telling me was so I wouldn't feel inadequate if it didn't happen. Well it did happen—twice. One year, two orgasms. (I think that still put me ahead of the curve.)

Mallory admitted she was so used to cumming from clitoral stimulation via her vibrator that it was extremely difficult for her to have an internal orgasm. She wasn't lying. (I suppose to be forewarned is to be foretold.) Three minutes alone with her vibrator and Mallory could be heard bellowing guttural noises that had my next-door neighbors high-fiving me the following morning, thinking I was the cause.

Pure pleasure aside, however, vibrator usage has been proven to benefit women in another positive way. Back in 2009, results of a survey funded by Church and Dwight Co., Inc., maker of Trojan brand sexual health products, indicated that female vibrator users were significantly more likely to have had a gynecological exam during the past year and to have performed genital self-examination during the previous month.[2]

According to these same studies, men (both gay and heterosexual) were also incorporating vibrators into their sexual activities. Of those who had used vibrators, 10 percent had done so in the past month, about 14 percent in the past year, and about 21 percent more than one year prior.

Men who reported having used vibrators, particularly those with more recent use, were more likely to report participation in sexual health-promoting behaviors, such as testicular self-exam. Men who had used vibrators indicated an increase in erectile function, intercourse satisfaction, orgasmic function, and sexual desire.

Despite these facts, I still had come to my own conclusion after watching the show. It seemed to me that by inventing a solution to solve a female problem, man had unintentionally helped create one of his own: blue balls. I mean, it was bad enough when we had to contend with age-old excuses like "Honey, I have a headache" or "It's that time of the month," in trying to get laid, but now, we are truly screwed—or not—

---

[2] Half of Americans Use Vibrators, Study Claims," *Live Science*,Live Science staff, June 29, 2009.

because man can pop as many performance- enhancing pills as he wants but he still won't outlast a fresh pair of AA batteries.

It could be argued that in some ways, the vibrator has contributed to the building of male sexual-inadequacy complexes by helping deconstruct the already fragile male ego. In other words, a brilliant concept backfired: In his genius, man invented a tool to cure woman of hysteria. In her genius, woman used that tool to drive herself into hysterics. Man's genius was thus turned against him. Woman is the true genius!

WHEN A STRANGER CALLS

Weird phone calls are a part of customer-service life at a porn shop. Some callers take advantage of the safety and anonymity the barrier provides to be rude and offensive—or just plain stupid. I liken those callers to zoo patrons who tap on the glass to get an animal's attention, ignoring the sign right above their heads: Please Don't Disturb the Animals. But they do anyway, because they can and they think it's funny. Before I worked in customer service, I'd seen footage of animals suddenly attacking unsuspecting bystanders and thought, How terrible! Now I think, I kinda get it!

A change in attitude brought about by conversations like the following.

One morning, the phone rang.

"Hello, this is André speaking. How may I help you?" (When I first started the job, I made a conscious effort to be as courteous and helpful as possible. Sometimes this was a good thing—other times ... not so much!)

On the other end of the phone, a gentleman spoke very softly. "Yes, I would like to know if you carry more than just videos at your store?"

The Marvel comics character Spider-Man (Peter Parker) is known for having a "spider sense" that alerts him to nearby suspicious activity. I have never been bitten by a radioactive spider—which is how Peter Parker derived his super powers—but my own early warning system was triggered. Perhaps it was because of the caller's low tone of voice, which was reminiscent of a nervous fifteen-year-old hiding beneath the covers while secretly talking to his girlfriend past bedtime or the cautious husband whispering just out of earshot of his wife while he conversed on the phone with another woman in the next room. In either case, the caller's true intent was cleverly disguised behind the legitimacy of his question, so I played along. "We carry all things adult," I responded, "magazines, lubes, lingerie, pills, toys."

Apparently, this was the magic word. "Toys!" he gleefully squealed. "What kind of toys?!"

I rattled off possible items of interest. "Cock rings, masturbators, vibrators, whips, hand-cuffs ...." He didn't respond, so I pressed on. "Sir, are you looking for something specific?"

"Aren't we all?" he replied coyly.

My spider sense was starting to tingle again.

"Does your store carry strap-ons?"

"Yes."

"The hollow ones where you can insert your penis?"

"... Yes."

"How big are they? I'm small, so I want to feel like I have a big dick."

That was too much information, but understandable. Every man wants to feel bionic in the bedroom—bigger, stronger, faster (making a woman cum, of course—but usually, men ask for enhancement pills or even penis extensions to achieve this end. Strap-ons are generally a lesbian tool of the sexual trade). Foolishly ignoring this clue, I continued to provide excellent customer service while making my second mistake.

"They come in different sizes," I said. "You would need to come to the store and see for yourself."

Once again the savvy caller exploited an opening left by the naive clerk. "Why, I would love to come to your store, sir. You have a very deep, sexy voice. May I ask your ethnicity?"

My spider sense was going berserk! A long, pregnant pause preceded my final miscalculated step, which led the unsuspecting hero right into the villainous trap. "What does that have to do with anything?" I asked.

"Well … I have been in your store a few times. I have *noticed* you behind the counter— even more so the *bulge* in your jeans! I have this fantasy about a black man taking me in a booth and having his way with me. You probably have a big dick, but I don't, so I would use the strap-on to return the favor!"

We had a web-slinger down! Unfortunately, unlike in the comic strip, this do-gooder was not afforded the luxury of waiting until the next issue to make a heroic comeback, so I had to regain—at least partially—my wits enough to muster a response. I had a flashback of my incident at the bar with Kat, but this was a different level of decimation. Whether I liked it or not, I was beginning to personify the saying, "It's not how many times you are knocked down but how many times you get up."

Rise, Spidey!

"Sir, if that is your impetus behind purchasing a strap-on, I'm afraid you've got the wrong man," I assured the caller. "Your offer is flattering, but the attempt is futile, I'm afraid."

There was no moral to this story, only immorality. At least, that is the way I interpreted it—but then I thought about the judgment in my assessment. Then I wondered, *Am I seriously having an internal dialogue about morality in a porn shop?* This would be the first of many more—even deeper—conversations I would have with myself in the future.

The experience did prove to be valuable, however. From then on, I learned to screen callers during a conversation by paying attention to subtle (and not-so-subtle) clues that would allow me to better gauge their intentions. And of course that weekend, I went out and bought even *baggier* jeans.

WHERE EVERYBODY KNOWS YOUR NAME

The sitcom Cheers has long been one of my favorite television shows. Before working at an adult store, I had never appreciated how a bar scene could so brilliantly capture such colorful and diverse characters, not to mention the functioning dysfunctional relationships they all shared.

The main character, Sam Malone, was more than just the head bartender. He was a buddy, friend, confidant, and psychologist to many of those who visited his establishment. I had always wondered how one man performing a simple task could be so many things to so many different people, but I would find my answer working behind a counter of my own.

Both bars and porn shops are places where people can go to relieve stress in ways they can-not in public. In both places, people can indulge (or overindulge) comfortably without fear of judgment. Both provide a safe environment where people can divulge extremely personal information to total strangers without concern of outside repercussions. It is no wonder, then, that during America's worst economic recessions, the two businesses that seem to still thrive are alcohol and pornography. People will drink. People will have sex.

People will drink and have sex.

I daresay, however, that the bond shared between clerk and customer can be even greater than that of bartender and boozer, my proof being in both the degree and amount of personal information shared. The hardest thing for a man to admit is that his sexual prowess is waning, but this is essentially what he is conceding to a clerk when he comes to the store in search of a product to boost his performance in the bedroom. On the flip side, when a female buys an item to be used below the waist, she is basically giving a clerk a glimpse into her private needs and desires.

No amount of liquid courage could work as quickly or be more effective than these simple transactions, which often lead into dialogue revealing more serious issues and topics.

Nonbelievers take one of my past encounters as an example.

"Hello, youngster," said a frumpy little man wearing oversized pants and an undersized tee shirt. "My name is Sparky. Can I get a bottle of pills? I have an old spinal injury, and they help me get it up."

Clerks often get unsolicited explanations like these from pill buyers because when a man's sexual performance begins to falter, his ego needs to provide adequate explanation—valid or otherwise— about why assistance is needed. Said ego is best satiated by a few strokes (no pun intended) of reassurance.

"Everyone needs reinforcements at some point," I told Sparky. "That's why you see this cabinet full of pills." To help shift the focus from his "problem" and thus avoid any feelings of discomfort or embarrassment on his part, I went straight to the sale. "That will be $10.79."

Sparky sped right through my red light. "You wouldn't believe it but, I'm a former crack addict! I have been stabbed and shot at for being around the wrong crowd trying to score!"

How would Sam Malone respond? I wondered. Although he didn't drink, as he was a recovering alcoholic, if Sam so chose, he could take advantage of the surplus of nearby alcohol. Unfortunately, there were no whiskey shots in arms reach for me, but I did have a bottle of vitamin water. It would have to do.

Sparky became more comfortable as he spoke, resting his elbows on the glass and placing his chin on the palms of his hands. My sales counter had become his shrink couch.

Sparky's thick fingers caressed the sides of his wrinkled face, which wore the ravages of time and drugs. "One day, I went to a crack house and was about to light up. I dropped my rock on the ground and couldn't find it. Suddenly, a woman squatted in front of me and peed. Right then, I realized I wasn't going to be one of those people my friends were talking about—I already was!"

It was not your conventional *Aha!* moment, but I was glad to hear this awakening had provided Sparky with the resolve he needed to walk away from his addiction. "I dropped the pipe and crushed it into the carpet like this," he said as he demonstrated. "I cleaned myself up, got a job as an electrician, and got married. That was fifteen years ago."

I flashed an encouraging smile, taking pride in Sparky's achievement; however, the gesture was a bit premature, as I soon learned he had moved on from one vice to another. "Now I am hooked on these pills!" Sparky said, shaking the bottle. "I am fifty- three years old and can stroke, and stroke, and pump for hours. My wife asks me, 'Are you done yet?' ... but my girlfriend says, 'You aren't done yet, are you?'"

Bewildered, I blurted, "Girlfriend?"

"Girlfriend!" he enthusiastically repeated. "And she is twenty-eight!"

I got the feeling that overcoming the drug habit took a distant second to his most recent accomplishment. Sparky was playing a numbers game: Twenty-five-year age difference trumps fifteen years clean and sober. Infidelity aside, here is a clear case of thinking with the wrong head.

"You two should make a movie," I jokingly suggested.

"Funny you should mention that," Sparky responded, proving I still hadn't learned when to keep my mouth shut. "We have talked about filming ourselves. How do I do that? Who do I contact? How much do they pay? I already have the video equipment!"

Incredulous, I was at a loss for words again—which was fast becoming a frequent occurrence— but I was saved by a male customer coming through the door in search of lingerie. Thankfully, Sparky took this as his cue. He gathered his things and headed out, waving his free hand. "I'll come back another time and maybe you will have some information for me."

I nodded.

About twenty minutes later, the same gentleman who had rescued me from Sparky's attention made his way to the counter holding two dresses and a pair of stockings. "Some lady is going to be very excited by these purchases," I told him. (It's funny how much friendlier I am during the last hour of my shift.)

He looked at me somewhat nervously, as if he were uncertain about the items he had picked out. This is normal male-buyer behavior, as choosing personal items for a woman can be a tricky endeavor. That's why I have never understood why women send guys to the porn store with the instructions "Get something I would like." Mission impossible!

Whatever the purchase, the guys frequently come back groaning, "She didn't like it!" The gentleman's hesitation was therefore understandable—if in fact, that had been the reason for his hesitation. But it wasn't, exactly.

Somberly, he began to recollect. "See, I had this girlfriend from Mexico who used to be my maid." I knew from the melancholy look on his face that this impromptu session could get lengthy and involved. (Always when my office hours are just about over.) "I would hit on her all the time while she was cleaning my apartment," he continued. "Finally, one day, she agreed to a date." (Always good to see persistence pay off at the expense of sexual harassment.) "Everything went well the first month even though I didn't get laid," he stated with disappointment in his voice. "I started getting antsy, plus she was asking for money to buy clothes and shoes. I figured it was a good investment that would pay off, eventually."

(Thinking with the wrong head, take two.)

"I noticed some mornings, she was really tired and wondered what she was doing at night, because I wasn't getting any action." His brow raised. "I know she had kids and had mentioned a night job. She would never let me take her home, though. I always dropped her off at the US-Mexico border crossing."

I felt like a seven-year-old being told his bedtime story. I started getting excited because I'd never heard the one about the international gold digger! The customer continued by telling me that on one Friday night, he had decided it was time, and he went across the border too. "I made up my mind to get drunk and find a hooker since she wasn't giving me any pussy."

The man had a point.

"A few hours later, I'm leaving this bar totally buzzed. As I'm 'walking' down the street, I notice a group of girls all lined up on a corner."

"Makes for convenient shopping," I added.

"I noticed a particular girl wearing a pretty purple dress and white stiletto heels. The outfit looked familiar—very familiar … it was her!" He slammed his hand emphatically on the counter, startling me momentarily. "She was being led off by some guy whose hand was palming the ass that I wasn't getting—in the dress that I paid for! I confronted her about it the next time I saw her, and she said, 'If you gave me more money, I wouldn't need my night job.'"

The woman had a point.

"Surely, you ended it then, right?" I presumed.

"Actually," he sheepishly replied, "I gave her a raise … but I finally got laid."

A mutually beneficial relationship between two people truly deserving of one another.

"Everything was good for a few weeks—until the evening I took her by my son's house. My son and I had a somewhat strained relationship for years, but we were sorting out our differences. When he came out to the car and saw her in the passenger seat, he angrily asked what I was doing with her!"

Oh boy, just when I thought it was safe to turn out the night-light!

"I told my son she was my new girlfriend and I was going to introduce them. Suddenly, my son's face was washed over with anger and he yelled, 'That woman performed at my friend's bachelor party and fucked half the guys in the room. If that is the company you keep, I don't want you in my life!'"

I think I need more vitamin water.

Dejectedly, he reached into his wallet, pulled out three crisp $20 bills, and handed them to me. "I haven't seen either of them since. That was about two weeks ago."

I calculated his change, bagged up his items, and attempted to complete the transaction on a positive note. "Well, everything is a learning experience." It was a weak attempt, indeed, but I was tired and out of vitamin water, and it was closing time. Realizing this, I quickly tried to rebound. "So are you going to see your son sometime soon—try and make amends?"

"Nope … and as you can see," he said, wagging the package of lingerie, "I have plans tonight."

"Oh, you found someone new, did you?"

"No. I'm off to Mexico to find the girl in my purple dress."

DIFFERENT FOLKS, SAME STROKES

More than a month had passed since I had heard it, but I still couldn't stop replaying the story in my mind about the maid/stripper/hooker—particularly the ending. As is often said, "The heart wants what it wants"—even though the head knows better. Whether this man was experiencing love or not, who was I to say? What I can speak on, however, is that every man at some point in his life is guilty of getting involved—romantically or otherwise—with the wrong woman.

Personally, I had experienced the female roommate who wanted to be more than friends. Nikki was her name—and she was no darlin'. She was convinced that if she showed me how different she was from the other women out there, I would "come to my senses" and want a relationship with her. The only thing she made me realize, however, was that one should never share an America Online account with a friend who has the master screen name. Because it was Nikki's computer and account, I suppose she felt it was her inalienable cyber right to meddle in my affairs as she pleased. She was signing in under my screen name and talking to the women on my friend list, all while pretending to be a naive house-wife who had discovered her husband was carrying on relationships with other unsuspecting females.

Based on the common greeting I received when I finally signed on, my screen name may as well have been Asshole. I had never known a person could be ostracized by people in a chat room—a place where many of the occupants were lying about their looks, income, or life in general. The greater irony was that I had not been disingenuous about any of those things.

Of course, when confronted, Nikki feigned ignorance, despite log-in times proving some-one had been on under my screen name. She even claimed to be insulted—not only be-cause I "had the nerve" to suggest duplicity on her part but that I would give credence to the words of those "crazy bitches" that I "didn't even know!"

I was beginning to understand, though, why sometimes in the middle of my late-night cyber chats, the computer would suddenly cut off. Coincidentally, the power cord was plugged into the wall in Nikki's room. She would always blame it on a bad connection and insisted that the same thing would happen to her, but it was strange how I seemed to experience this problem only when I was laughing and obviously enjoying a conversation—and when she was home.

Just like that lingerie-buying customer, however, I too had set reason aside, allowing myself to be duped into believing that Nikki wouldn't betray our friendship in such a manner.

Like the song says, "Everybody Plays the Fool." The adage "Absolute power corrupts absolutely" also comes to mind. Traditionally, this is an unfortunate consequence befalling great men of authority, but thanks to the advent of role reversal, I suppose it can now be applied to the modern woman as well.

I pondered all of this as I leaned against the store counter. Suddenly, my wayward thoughts were cut short by the familiar click of the door being opened. It took a few seconds for me to refocus my attention from past events to present time, so I caught only a glimpse of the customer at first, but quickly, the hazy image of a tall, muscularly built man began to crystallize.

His stride was precisely measured, as if walking to a cadence, and his posture perfect.

He was military. An officer, I guess.

Visibly uncomfortable, he said, "I don't know if I should be wearing this shirt in here?"

His sculpted torso stretched out a blue tee shirt with "NAVY" spelled out in gold lettering across the chest.

Ironically, other members of the armed forces I'd encountered had not shared this officer's reservations. This type of timidity is completely lost on Marines, for example, who bring laser-like focus and a task-driven mentality to the purchasing process. Jarheads couldn't care less who sees them. In fact, they will kick the ass of anyone who has a problem with them being in a porn shop. *Ooh- Rah!*

An Army brat dressed in full fatigues had once stormed the store in search of a specific item for someone. "Hello, sir!" she greeted me. "I wasn't sure what time you guys closed, so I came straight from work."

"I can see that."

"I need your help with something. ... I must get a gel vibrator for my lesbian friend. She's in the Navy."

"I believe I can assist you with that."

We walked over to the wall, and I picked out a customer favorite. "This one should do the trick," I said. "It's soft at the base and along the tip, but sturdy in the middle where the motor is."

"Fuck yeah!" she shouted. "You are the man!" (Too bad all my customers aren't this appreciative!) "They aren't supposed to have these on the boat, but what does the Navy expect officers to do?!"

I shrugged my shoulders.

"Horny men and women around each other for months at a time.

You are either going to fuck or find something to fuck, right!" I nodded.

"I also need a box of condoms. I mean, you always need condoms, right?"

Another nod.

"I'm going to send her *this*, too." She grabbed a vibrating bullet off its hook. "My friend told me she didn't use bullets, and I asked her, 'What kind of lesbian are you?'"

Indeed.

As I rang up and bagged her items, she remarked, "You must meet some pretty interesting people in this store?"

I glanced up at her.

"Present company included," she laughed as she walked out.

When I thanked her for her business and service to the country, she responded, "Thank you for your service. Your industry is a lot better than mine!"

Those words would never have come out of my mouth, but she may have been on to something.

With my Naval friend who was a bit uneasy about being in the porn store, I kidded, "If you spend over $20, I won't alert your superiors."

He belted out a hearty laugh as his eyes continued to wander around the store. "I'm from Missouri, and this is a helluva climate change!" he acknowledged. "I was up in the Great Lakes area from November 'til February. I can see why so many people like it here!"

"Yeah ... the weather is pretty good, too!"

He cracked another smile while peering through the glass counter, carefully inspecting the contents. "Let me have two of your enhancement pills." Flipping through his wallet, he pulled out his credit card and identification. "Do you give military discounts?"

"We don't give employees discounts." "Seriously?"

"I wouldn't lie to a man in uniform."

We both laughed.

"You'd be surprised how many times I get asked that question," I told him.

"You get a lot of military in here?"

"I'll put it to you like this: One would think by now, the word would have gotten around the ships that Video Expo does not give military discounts!"

"Wow!" was his only response as he nervously scribbled his signature on the credit-card printout.

"If only the Navy knew how many out-of-uniform officers frequent the store," I said. "Come around again and you might bump into someone you know." That was the wrong thing to say. He was officially triggered!

"Oh, no! Well, you have a good day, sir, and thanks for the assistance!" The ship left port *quickly*!

No sooner had he walked away than my mind started to wander again. The armed services accounted for some of our most loyal customers—and for good reason. Out on deployment, alone at sea, what's a guy or girl to do? Yep, *masturbate*! It's Sexual Survival 101!

And once our brave men and women touch down on American shores, their search begins for the *real* thing!

An episode of Sex and the *City* came to mind in which Carrie, Samantha, Charlotte, and Miranda go out on the town during Fleet Week, a United States Navy, Marine Corps, and Coast Guard tradition in which active military ships recently deployed in overseas operations dock in a variety of major cities for five days. Samantha, the carefree sexpot of the bunch, is admiring the scenery around her. "Oh my!" she shouts gleefully. "There's seamen everywhere!"

Miranda, the sexual conservative, looks at Carrie and murmurs under her breath, "When I turn around, there had better be sailors behind us!"

A few minutes after the officer left, that's when the homophone hit me: *seaman/semen*.

They are spelled slightly different but sounding the same, and they are similar in purpose:

They both travel long distances, navigating through harrowing canals to engage the target.

This type of determination deserves some type of reward, in my opinion, either monetarily (via a discount) or *certainly* emotionally in the form of freedom to shop guilt-free. Neither the former (thanks to store policy) nor the latter was possible, because of a judgmental, hypocritical society.

Out in society, the customer who had just left is seen as a military officer, but what we see as clerks is a person who is enlisted in the military. *Our* basic training teaches us to look at the individual *first!* (It's amazing how a place so widely stigmatized is one place that doesn't stigmatize!)

Though our professions may differ in life, the drive to satisfy our basic human needs remains the same. It is ironic that in a culture where we emphasize celebrating our differences, it is our similarities that truly teach us what it is to be human.

WHO YOU GONNA CALL?

There is not a more soothing early morning sound than that of silence. It is truly a welcome relief when you work in a noise-filled environment including everything from a bill breaker rumbling as it dispenses money to animalistic moans and groans echoing throughout the store hallways.

Peace and quiet make the perfect pair, even more so than peanut butter and jelly, the Fourth of July and fireworks, and Batman and Robin. Speaking of the Dynamic Duo, I realized I could probably use their assistance with the character stumbling out of the bathroom. (I swear, good times never last for long!)

Wearing just pants and shoes, a man seemingly half-awake meandered his way to the counter with an empty packet of lube. "I need more," he bellowed, his torso glistening in the light.

"I think the idea is to get it all over your *hands*," I said. "Any chance that a shirt slid off somewhere along your pathway?"

"Yeah, it's in my booth—I like to get really comfortable." (Booths are rooms used for private viewing of videos.)

"You know, what would make me really comfortable is if that shirt found its way back on your body!" Breasts are desirable in a chicken dinner or on a woman, but on a man, not so much!

I told him the lube would cost him $1.08. That's when he tossed it on the counter, my biggest pet peeve: a crinkled wet bill. Creepily, it began to unfold like a blossoming flower via time-lapse photography. I cringed at the thought of the fluids likely saturating that little piece of green paper. Then came the coins! *Slimy* ... and *stuck* together.

I fired up the Bat-Signal for my personal dynamic duo, a pair of latex gloves. Then I realized the problem with this temporary solution was that I would still be putting money in the drawer now, only to deal with the disgust later, so I decided to eliminate any future trauma. "You can keep the change," I told him. It was only eight cents.

"Cool, brother," he responded. "I appreciate it." He thought I was doing *him* the favor!

After the transaction, out came the hand sanitizer (every clerk's best friend). I made a mental note to warn Sal, the general manager, about the possible unsavory condition of Booth 3, temporary dwelling place of Mr. I'm-Too-Sexy-for-My-Shirt.

Sal came around twice a week to gather the money from the bill breaker and inside the booths. He was a headstrong, feisty Italian in his mid-fifties. When asked how long he had been on the job, Sal's general response was "Too fuckin' long!" (There was something humorously apropos about an outspoken 5'6" gentleman with roots dating back to the Old Country coming around to collect the trappings of our success.)

Sal was expected in about fifteen minutes, which gave me some time to run to the restroom.

I passed Booth 3 enroute and smelled something burning. The door was ajar, and the room was dark save the light from the monitor—and one tiny scented candle. This guy had taken mood setting to another level! All for an intimate encounter with his favorite hand.

Call me a killjoy, but I told him, "Sorry, you are going to have to put out that candle."

"Aww, man!"

"I know, I know. The best-laid plans ..."

"Why do I have to put it out?"

"It's called a fire hazard."

After partially ruining his date, I resumed my trek to the bathroom. Just then, of course, the phone rang.

Fuckin' phone! It's like these people have radar! Not a single call for the last forty-five minutes, but once I need to take a whiz, somebody out there has a question. After stomping back to the front—my inner child fully channeled—I snatched the receiver off the wall. "Hello!" I grumbled. "Video Expo, how may I help you?"

On the other end, I heard an adorable little girl. "Hello, sir, I want to know if you have *Finding Nemo 2*?"

I *melted*. Women usually reference that term when describing the effect a voice can have on them emotionally. Let's just say at that moment, I was very much in touch with my feminine side and fully understood this concept. No longer was I worried about the half-naked guy sprawled out on the booth bench in his best Playgirl pose. Not even going to the bathroom was a concern. My thoughts had been hijacked by the sweetest voice I had heard in years. (Don't forget where I work.)

But wait! She didn't know this was a porn shop! *We seriously need to think about changing our store title*. I wasn't about to be the bearer of bad news—that was her parents' job. "So, is your mom around?" I asked her.

"Yes," she responded politely. "Would you like to speak to her, sir?"

"Please, can you get her for me?"

"Sure, hold on."

At that moment, the door swung open and Sal strutted through. "Hey, André!" he shouted. "How are we doing, today?"

"You know, Sal—another day in paradise!" With that, he disappeared to the back.

"Yes, hello!" a mature voice on the other end of the phone greeted me.

"Uh, yes, hello, ma'am." Gently, I tried to break the news to Mom. "Obviously, I didn't want to tell this to your daughter, but ... this is an X-rated establishment." Now picture a *Looney Tunes* cartoon, a glimpse inside the character's head revealing a tiny mouse frantically scrambling on a spinning wheel trying to capture an unattainable piece of cheese.

This would be the perfect visual of this mother's mind attempting to grasp a concept just beyond its comprehension. The mere fact that her daughter had called a porn shop was momentarily too heavy a burden for her to bear. Dialing the number was bad enough. But to make matters worse, her daughter had actually *talked* to someone! The young girl's sweet, innocent soul had been sullied. Her (not-yet- developed) reputation was forever tarnished. Eve had bitten the fruit!

Mom, finally able to form words, was not taking the news well.

She shrieked, "Oh my God, no!"

"Ma'am, your daughter has no idea," I reassured her. "I didn't mention anything to her."

It didn't matter. Mom's mood quickly turned from disbelief to displeasure—which was clearly displayed by her tone and volume. "Why didn't you just tell her that you don't carry the movie?" she snapped.

Unappreciative of her misplaced anger, I fired back, "What if I had said that and your daughter in return asked what movies we do have? Then what? Saying nothing seemed to be the best option. I think any conversation regarding this establishment is best left between a mother and her young daughter, not a store clerk and a little girl."

Claws retracted. "Perhaps, you're right," she begrudged me.

"Thank you."

Meanwhile, in the background, I heard a little girl quickly succumbing to her growing excitement. "What movies do they have, Mommy?! Huh? Do they have my movie? Do they?"

"Good luck, Mom!" I said to myself as I hung up the phone. Now, there was something I had been meaning to do. Ah, yes, the bathroom! I grabbed the keys, stepped from behind the counter, and briskly walked back toward the restroom. I passed the customer who had been in Booth 3. Now fully dressed, he headed toward the exit. It figures. Now he wants to wear a shirt.

Wait a minute, Sal came into the store, right? Oh yeah, I need to warn him about—"Motherfucker!"

Shit!

Sal was screaming out some of his best *"Italian."* I was too late to warn him, and he was not happy. *Always write down the reminder, Dré!* I quickly did an about-face and headed back to the safety and comfort of my chair. Next, I heard a loud thud and the glass marquee that displayed the movies playing inside the booths shook violently. The words I heard next were somewhat garbled, but I did recognize a few of the more colorful ones.

"Son of a bitch," Sal barked. "I can't believe these fuckers!" He turned out of the room and cut across to the other side of the store, where the remaining booths awaited him.

This gave me some much-needed time to gather myself before he came to the front. The last thing I wanted was to incur his wrath by giggling at his misfortune—not to mention, it was kind of my fault.

Sal started walking toward me, but I stayed focused on the sheet of paper I was using to note what supplies we needed. I doubled up on items we already had, as my intention was to avoid making eye contact for as long as possible to keep from laughing.

When the moment of truth finally came, I lied through my teeth. "I've been back in the supply room compiling a list of things we're running low on. How's everything going?"

More Italian. Sal flung the bag full of money onto the counter and pumped globs of sanitizer in his palm. "I wish I could put this fuckin' shit all over my body! I tried to sit down in front of the bill collector and damn near slid to the other end of the bench because it was covered in lube," he complained while shaking his hands feverishly in attempts to air-dry them. "I open the machine to pull out the bills— and the top stack is wet and sticky!"

Playfully, I pull out the box of gloves. "For next time?" I asked, subtly attempting to defuse the situation.

Sal's forehead was no longer wrinkled, and his jaw unclenched, both indicators that his anger was subsiding. He slid the box to the side. "Fuck gloves—I need a latex suit!" From there, he picked up his story. "I got up too quickly to get the hell out of that booth and lost my footing. It's like a damn ice arena! I reached out to brace myself, but my hand just slid down the wall and I fell on my ass!"

That would be the *thud* I'd heard.

Sal was wearing new contacts, he said, and the left one was causing irritation and blurred vision. That isn't a good combination when one is walking into a dimly lit, spatially challenged germ pool.

Fumbling through his pockets for keys, Sal made a discovery. "Look at this shit!" His left pant leg was soiled with a rather noticeable stain. "You got the number to Ghostbusters?"

"I've been slimed!"

"Fuck Ghostbusters!" I countering with some "Italian" of my own. "That looks like a job for hazmat!"

STRAYS

I was sharing the story about the youngster who was sleeping with his girlfriend's mom with a friend, Shari. She couldn't believe there were people like that in the world, and I couldn't believe she couldn't believe it. "They really aren't any different than your doctor, mailman, or next-door neighbor," I told her. "You'd be shocked to learn the things people you know do when no one is around. You only see what they want to reveal."

"If I found out my doctor visited places like that," Shari said, sitting upright on her couch, "I would change doctors."

"Well, if it were your gynecologist, it may be a tad awkward." "Ya think?!"

"But even so, it's not like he is about to grab a dildo to use on you. And if he is doing his job, what difference does it make how he chooses to spend his free time?"

"Oh, hell no!" she protested, wagging her finger. "While I'm spread-eagle, he could be thinking about some movie he just finished watching. I am not trying to be some perverted doctor's real-life fantasy."

Sensing another opening, I seized the opportunity. "No need to worry. Gynecologists generally go for the anal flicks. They see enough pussy during the week!"

Appalled, she shrieked, "Eww, gross," burying her face in her hands out of embarrassment. "That's disgusting!"

I laughed sadistically at her reaction, finding humor in her discomfort. "How could you work in a place like *that*?"

There was the judgment.

I didn't mind it so much anymore, because I was used to it, not to mention that before I had become a clerk, I had shared somewhat similar feelings about porn shops and people who frequented them, but one valuable lesson I had taken away from my sixteen-month adult education was that stereotyping and hypocrisy often go hand in hand. My time at the shop had proven it about me, and now I intended to prove it about Shari, so I got comfortable, slid back, and sank further into the sofa. I crossed my legs and looked across the glass magazine table that separated us, then smirked as I intentionally exaggerated my next word. "So-o-o ... you mean to tell me that if I went into your room and looked in your nightstand drawer, underneath your pillow, or in a shoebox tucked away in the back of the closet, I wouldn't find some sort of self-pleasuring device?"

Shari glanced up at the ceiling. Her foot tapped nervously against the floor. Blood rushed to her cheeks, now a rosy red. Incriminating evidence. *Guilty!*

Too much time had passed for a denial, and she knew it, so she offered her best rebuttal. "Well, see ... there is a difference." She waved her hands for emphasis while fighting back giggles. "I'm not like those people!"

That was vague, so I quickly challenged her statement. "That answer doesn't explain how you are different from those people!"

"They're gross!"

"Opinion."

"I have the decency to do what I do in the privacy of my own home!"

"They have the decency to do what they do in the privacy of their own booths."

"Yeah, but you know that sometimes there is more than one person in those booths!"

"Oh, so you're going to hang your hat on a multiple-partners argument?" I rearranged myself in the cushions, winding up for another haymaker. "While we're on the subject, didn't someone in this room *not* named Dré have a ménage à trois a few months ago?"

Shari was getting irritated, perhaps realizing she was more like *those* people than she cared to admit. "I see where you're going with this, but I'm not like them!" she insisted.

"Whatever helps you sleep at night—besides that vibrator!"

A pillow whizzed past my head. "Shut up!"

Out on the back porch, I heard a meow. This came as a surprise, because Shari's relationship with cats was strained, at best, since her mother's feline had scratched her above the eye when she was seven years old. A scar that remains.

"When did you re-acknowledge the existence of cats?" I asked, both stunned and intrigued. "You hate cats!"

"I know. That one was caught out in the rain one night, crying under my porch." A look of sympathy fell across her face. "The next morning it was still there, shaking, so I put some food out. Now I can't get rid of her."

I broke the news to her. "She's yours! Or should I say, you're hers!

A similar dynamic exists at work, but with a slight twist." "Dré, you have strays at your job?"

"Oh yes! The difference is, they try to feed me!"

Shari folded her arms. "As you would say, this should be good." "If you don't want a stray animal around your property, the worst thing you can do is feed it. And not unlike its domesticated counterpart, the stray will also become reliant upon that action which satisfies its most basic need."

"So I'm pretty much screwed?"

"Pretty much! The bowl of food establishes a bond between giver and receiver, whether it be human-animal or human-human. Yours was simply a random act of kindness; however, when a customer does this, the motive is self-serving."

"How so?"

"Their purpose is to disarm," I explained, "dull your keen sense of suspicion and, in effect, cause you to lower your guard around them."

"Seriously. They play mind games like that?"

"You have no idea! Some of them will come to expect preferential treatment depending upon what they bring or how much they give you."

Shari was a bit incredulous. "Oh my god, really? Over some food!"

"Why the surprise? Men have been bonding over food since cavemen first started sharing their kills," I pointed out. "Besides, you know the saying, 'The way to a man's heart …'"

"Is through his stomach!"

I explained to her that with most customers, the best thing to do when offered food was to say no, because once that clearly defined line between clerk and customer becomes blurred into clerk and comrade, it lends itself to rules being bent and all sorts of other problems.

It was then Shari's turn to interrogate. "So you're saying if I brought you a sandwich and salad for lunch, you wouldn't take it?"

"Not the salad, because I don't care for them." I paused briefly. "And not if you were expecting to get a discount on another pair of handcuffs…"

"What?! Wait a minute. How did you know I had handcuffs?"

"I didn't, but you're right—you're nothing like those people!"

BIRDS OF A FEATHER

It's already been established that sharing a meal is a prime example of male bonding.

Enjoying an alcoholic beverage while swapping stories or watching a popular sporting event—particularly football or boxing— is another. There is one male ritual that trumps all others, however. It is an activity familiar to every man—one that he will experience several times, if not all throughout his life: commiserating over relationship mishaps.

That was how Terrence—a customer who became a good friend—and I became close. We were wounded soldiers in the "war of the roses," two damaged peas in a pod. We bonded over our triumphs and tragedies in the arena of love. We laughed. We bitched. We moaned. We eased each other's pain.

Eventually, we recognized our mistakes—and with those realizations came understanding. Initially, however, as is customary with all jilted lovers, came the complaints. "I used to date this girl named Penelope, and I should have known from her name alone that she would be high-maintenance," Terrence said. "But I met her at church, so, you know, I was thinking she was sweet and innocent."

Terrence was a writer like I was, screenplays being his forte. He always toted around a worn black leather satchel containing scribbled notes of various projects in the works. He was upbeat and very animated, his voice rising a pitch or two whenever he became excited.

Politics and world events were among his favorite topics of discussion—second only to women.

"After our first date, I remember pulling up to her house to drop her off." Terrence laid his bag against the counter and readjusted his hat. "We had a really nice dinner and great conversation." He then scratched his head, trying to wrap his mind around what he would tell me next. "She leaned over and gave me a kiss. So I kissed her back. She grabbed my hand and placed it on her breast and she put her hand on my crotch."

Raising an eyebrow, I responded, "Those church girls really know how to play hard to get."

"Oh man! That's not the craziest part—she leaned over and whispered in my ear, 'I need $75 to get my hair done.'"

He burst into laughter, and I soon followed.

"I guess if she had put your hand on *her* crotch, that would have cost $125 to cover the manicure and pedicure, too," I surmised. "So what happened?"

"You mean *after* I went limp?"

More laughter.

"I couldn't believe it!" Terrence said. "It would be less of a shock if I had met her at a club—but church?"

"Church is the new club!" I informed him. "Have you seen the outfits some women wear to service? At some places of worship, it's hard to tell if it's Sunday morning or Saturday night!"

"I guess they try to catch a hot guy, then the holy ghost!"

"Amen, brutha!"

"She threw my shit all off, though, André!"

"I bet."

"After that, I didn't go out on a date for months." Once Terrence had finished shaking his head, he asked me, "Have you ever experienced anything that crazy?"

I tilted my head sideways and shot Terrence the are-you-kidding-me? look. "How much time ya got?" I said.

He smiled, then clapped his hands and rubbed them together. "Okay, go ahead and top that!"

"When I was in Los Angeles, I met this girl off a chat line," I began. Embarrassingly, I had to dig through my archive of most-forgettable moments. "She was a college student living in Santa Monica. We agreed to meet for lunch at a nearby restaurant. Since she didn't have transportation, I offered to pick her up at her apartment."

Terrence was always attentive when we shared stories and we were bemused by the other's dating disasters. He rubbed his hands together again. "I can tell this is going to be good!"

"She was a petite little Asian girl," I continued. "Olive-skinned with long black hair that reached the small of her back. Barely over five feet tall and one hundred pounds soaking wet."

Terrence drank in the description. "Ooh ... she sounds beautiful!

Like a delicious little appetizer."

"She cost like a seven-course meal, though!"

"Uh-oh!"

"*Uh*-oh is right!"

"I think I know where you're going, Dré. I used to date this girl who was Filipino and Malaysian. She looked like a porcelain doll. Very high-maintenance."

"This girl's metabolism was high-maintenance," I griped. "The more she ate—the lighter my wallet got!"

"See, that's where guys make their mistake," Terrence deduced. "Ain't nothing wrong with going dutch when you don't know about a girl's eating habits."

"This girl brought a buffet appetite to a four-star sushi restaurant," I said. "She played that starving-student role. I ignored all the signs and ran smack-dab into a brick wall!"

"André, you have to pay attention to the red flags!"

"I know. Now that I think about it, she even went as far as to say guys should have to pay for her company!"

Aghast, Terrance remarked, "I'm surprised you didn't turn around right there and walk away!"

"I admit, I thought about it. As a matter of fact, looking back, I should have. But at the time, I was thirty minutes away from home and I was starving! You know a man can't think straight when he's hungry!" The more I remembered about that evening, the more I wanted to forget. It wasn't one of my prouder bachelor moments, but it served its purpose as a learning experience and a bonding moment to share.

"We finally decided on a place, went in, and sat down," I recalled. I found myself taking a seat behind the counter as I talked. "From the start, she began quizzing the waiter about the contents of the different sushi roles."

"What? Why?"

"Supposedly, she had sensitivities to certain ingredients—which I can understand. But she had the waiter going back and forth to the kitchen to ask the cook about his food preparation. Soon, the waiter got flustered and the cook came out because he was now agitated."

"Oh man!"

"Brilliant idea to piss off the guy preparing our food, right?! It took twenty minutes for her to order five sushi rolls along with a large Chinese chicken salad and a coke. Of course, while she waited, she had to get an appetizer—hot and spicy buffalo wings."

"Let me guess, you just had a burger and fries, right?"

"Close. I think it was a chicken breast sandwich. All I know is my portion came to around $11 and hers was already up to $40. First she was annoying, then inconsiderate—and she was just getting started."

"It gets worse?"

"I'd only brought $60 dollars with me, thinking that would be plenty. Once I realized the bill was already close to that—not including the tip—I thought it best to run to the ATM, so before I left the restaurant, I gave the waiter specific instructions."

"Which were?"

"Don't bring any more food to this table!"

"How can a girl that small put away that much food?" Terrence wondered. "She probably couldn't afford to eat like that on her own, so she overindulged when she went out on dates."

"Probably."

I recalled how I had zipped out that restaurant door, footing through boulevard traffic: skateboarders, dog-walkers and street-performers ranging from a talented youngster drumming on two overturned plastic containers to a transplanted hippie playing sixties tunes on a banjo. Third Street Promenade in Santa Monica can be a wonderful outing—with the right company.

"About eight minutes later, I got to the ATM machine and realized I had a slight problem," I remembered.

Terrence slapped his forehead. "Oh no!"

"Oh yes! I'd left the damn card at home. Now I'm heated! It's commonplace in LA to see people walking around talking to themselves, so I'm sure passersby just labeled me among the crazy!"

"Only a woman can make a man that mad," Terrence declared. "I've been so angry; I remember almost being hit by a bus because I wasn't paying attention crossing the street. If you see a guy walking around shaking his head and talking to himself, chances are he's having female problems!"

"I didn't think I could be any more upset, but sure enough, I was proven wrong when I got back to the restaurant and saw this girl eating more food!"

"What?!"

"Yes! I couldn't believe it, so I went into the kitchen to scream at the first person I saw! That happened to be the manager."

I pointed at our table. "Why is there more food over there?" I asked rather tersely. "I told the waiter before I left to only bring the check!"

"You need to talk to your girlfriend!" she fired back. "She keeps ordering food."

"She isn't cooking it, is she?! Now I don't have enough money to cover the bill."

Those words got her to stop her busyness long enough to glare my way. "So how do you plan to pay?"

"Time to bust some suds!" Terrence joked. "You should have paid for your portion and let her wash dishes to pay for hers."

It's true. It was during times like those that I regretted not inheriting the asshole gene. "So what did you do, André?" Terrence asked.

"I paid what I could, left my driver's license, and returned the next day with the remainder."

"What about your date?"

"What about her?"

"Was that the last time you saw her?"

"Yup. When I dropped her off, she said she enjoyed the date and wanted to go out again. I looked at her like she had three heads, and burned rubber!"

"Yours was good, but I think mine had more shock value," Terrence boasted. "I mean, you wouldn't expect that type of behavior from a churchgoing girl—and on the first date!"

"I can top both of you," a raspy voice proclaimed. Apparently, a customer had been listening in on our conversation. "I didn't mean to eavesdrop, but the stories were great! However, I've got one even better!"

Men always must one-up each other. It's a familiar game as well as long-standing tradition:

Who can get the most phone numbers? Who has the faster car?

Who's more well-endowed?

It's what we do. It's who we are. So, with the gauntlet laid down, the challenge was accepted.

Terrence glimpsed at me. I nodded and gave the gentleman the floor. "Okay, sir. Let's hear it."

"Once upon a time, I was married." He raised his left hand, exposing a ring finger that sported no jewelry, only a lightened imprint of a broken promise. "I was running around on my old lady." Other shoppers in the store must have caught on to our game, because the once scattered crowd seemed to have gathered near the counter.

"The mistress decided she no longer wanted to be second best," he said, "so she threatened to tell my wife about our affair. I called her bluff and decided to break it off. She informed me it wasn't going to be as easy as that after being involved for two years."

Terrence was the first to verbalize what we were all thinking—what every man thinks when he is caught in a love triangle in which the other woman becomes acrimoniously dissatisfied with her role. "Fatal attraction," Terrence diagnosed.

"Yeah, I hope you didn't have any pet rabbits," someone cracked.

"Do you know, that bitch called my wife and told her everything! I mean, she gave her dates, times, even told her the made-up excuses I used to sneak out and see her!"

"What did you expect?" I asked. "You know the saying, 'Hell hath no fury like a woman scorned!' And you pissed off two of them!"

"As my pops used to say, 'It's cheaper to keep her.'" Terrence added. "Obviously, that applies to the wife and the mistress."

"True," the customer acquiesced. "They weren't done, though. The wife divorced me and took half of everything I owned. The mistress moved in with her—and now they are lovers!"

"Damn!" I shouted. "I wasn't expecting that!" Quickly, I turned to my surroundings for help putting things into perspective. "This story needs to be a porno, except in the end, you go back to the house and have a threesome—then they kick you out!"

He smiled at the idea. "I would have settled for that kind of happy send-off."

Terrence looked at me. "Dré, our stories were good, but he gets king of the day for that one!"

"Congratulations!" I told the guy. "You earned that title, buddy. Painfully so!"

RAP, ROCK, RESPECT

When my coworkers learned I used to be a journalist, specifically one who wrote stories for the LA Times, it seemed I became the resident know-it-all on all I was the sports authority. Everyone looked to me as a voice of reason whenever troubling news hit the airwaves, even though I told them I had never been good about keeping up with current events, and if the correct spelling or meaning of a word was needed, I was both Google and Wikipedia.

Though I never claimed to be an expert in any area, the fact that my opinion was so valued did mean a lot to me, especially because my dismissal from the Times had left me feeling unwanted and unappreciated. Recalling some of my journalistic exploits with friends at work proved to be somewhat therapeutic in helping me remember what I loved about writing.

A young man named Chris proved to be instrumental in this endeavor. He was a nineteen-year-old hire not far removed from high school, and though our ages and ethnicities—he was Caucasian—differed greatly, we shared common ground on many topics. Our discussions of one in particular—music—would help kick-start my healing process.

"Who is this we are listening to on the radio?" I asked Chris one day at the store. He was still in training, and I was responsible for showing him the ropes. Apparently, it would also be my job to educate him on the history of good music.

"This is Da Baby," he responded. "Do you like him?"

"Never listened to him, really. I don't care much for the commercial hip-hop music that's out these days because it all sounds the same to me."

"You think so, huh?" Chris took a moment and then started throwing names of popular artists at me. "What about Drake ... do you like him?"

"Yeah, I like some of his music, but once he got popular, the radio became saturated with anyone who sounded like him. And hip-hop today seems to be all about drinking bottles of champagne, sleeping with multiple women, and spending money as fast as you can earn it. With everything going on today, you mean to tell me that's all there is to talk about?"

"You like Megan Thee Stallion.?"

"You ever heard of Lil' Kim or Foxy Brown?"

"Who?"

Shaking my head, I uttered, "Kids today."

Chris believed music was generational and so listeners tend to think the music they grew up with is always the best. "My pops always tells me about how the music he listened to in his day had a message and the artists stood for something."

"Your dad grew up in, what, the sixties?" I guessed.

"Yup."

I nodded my head in agreement with Chris's father's statement. "Your dad, then, is one hundred percent correct! The music then poignantly reflected the mood of the times. It captured the essence of arguably the most important decade of the twentieth century in terms of social and political change. That's why I loved hip-hop in the late eighties and early nineties. It did the same thing from the perspective of the young black youth."

Chris laughed. "Man, I was barely born around that time."

I sighed, realizing I had dated myself. "Scary, isn't it."

"Public Enemy was big back then, right?" Chris asked.

"Yes, they were," I answered. "They were one of the militant arms of the 'Afro-centric movement' rap was going through."

"What was that about?"

"Enlightenment, basically. Educating blacks on our history and encouraging us to help ourselves, to get along with one another, and to be proud of who we are as a people."

Chris pondered his next question for a moment, not wanting to seem naïve. "Okay, this may sound stupid, but—N.W.A. wasn't a part of that movement, right?"

That time, I laughed. "Not exactly, although N.W.A.'s music was definitely enlightening and informative! They were talking about what was going on in the hood."

"What's that one song they did?" Chris asked me while snapping his fingers to help jog his memory. "Oh yeah, 'Fuck Tha Police'!"

Our conversation was starting to send me back into a time I had not entered in nearly twenty years. "That was a sentiment shared by many in Los Angeles during the time that song was released," I remembered.

"There was another song about the police that came out back then too," Chris continued. "It was by Ice-T! But I can't remember the name."

"Perhaps you should snap your fingers again."

"C'mon, man! You should definitely know this stuff!"

"Why, because I'm old?"

"Well, that too! But naw, this was your musical era!"

"The song you are referring to is called 'Cop Killer.'"

"That's right! 'Cop Killer'! Did you like it?"

"I never really listened to 'Cop Killer' because it was a hardcore metal song with a lot of yelling and screaming. However, the record holds tremendous sentimental value for me."

"Really? Why?"

Wow! I was about to open a door that had been mentally sealed shut for as long as I could remember. Talking about this would require me to sift through some serious baggage.

Maybe this was the universe's way of telling me I needed to finally let go of some things.

Or perhaps it was nothing that profound, simply a youngster asking a question. Whichever the case, I obliged. "Well, Chris," I opened up, "one of the first stories I ever wrote was about this song— and it was my very first story talking about a major celebrity."

"Cool! What publication was it in?"

"The Poynter Press."

"The what? Never heard of it!"

"I'm not surprised. A group of students made up the name."

"What students? Where? Did you meet Ice-T? What was he like?"

It was all coming back to me. Chris' rapid-fire questions triggered feelings of anxiety, frustration, and excitement all at once. I wanted to give him answers, but there was too much to discuss in so little time, so I surmised a way to kill his four birds with the proverbial single stone. "Chris, I'm pretty sure I have a copy of the story lying around my apartment somewhere. I'll bring one tomorrow, and we can pick up where we left off."

"That sounds good! I'm going to go put these movies away and clean up in the back before I leave. Don't forget the paper tomorrow!"

"I won't."

When I got home, finding the article was the easy part. I kept all of my writings and publications inside a family of boxes at the back of my closet. The hard part was opening the containers and dealing with all the emotions that sprang forth.

After about an hour's worth of laughter—and tears—I had gathered a few newspapers to take to Chris, including the "Cop Killer" story. I spent the remainder of the night reading and reminiscing.

Good therapy!

The next morning, Chris came charging through the door smiling like the Joker, unable to bridle his enthusiasm. "Do you have it?" he screamed. "Did you bring it?"

Because Chris resembled the Clown Prince of Crime, it was only appropriate then that I imitate the calm, cool, and collected Caped Crusader. I mumbled, "I got 'em," in my throatiest Batman voice. Despite my stoic exterior, inside, I was nervously excited to have someone read one of my stories again.

"Lemme see!" Chris demanded.

"You might want to clock in first," I suggested.

"Oh yeah, huh? Good idea." After doing so, Chris grabbed the stack of papers lying on the counter. "Which one is it?"

"The one on top."

He marveled at the cover and the graphic illustration of Ice-T, who was wearing shades and a black ski hat and brandishing an Uzi submachine gun. Chris began thumbing through the paper. Interestingly enough, the publication I had brought in seemed to create more questions than it provided answers.

"So what is this Poynter?" Chris questioned. "Funny name."

"But a fantastic institution! Hands down, my time at the Poynter was one of the best experiences of my life!" I explained to Chris that the Poynter Institute was an organization that offered a six-week summer fellowship to twenty fortunate would-be writers and graphic illustrators. During the course, students would be introduced to and instructed on all facets of journalism, and other writers, copy editors, and graphic artists from select newspapers all across the country would periodically stop by to provide expert tutelage.

There were Monday-morning group meetings to discuss story ideas. Writers and graphic artists were then paired up to work on these stories during the week in preparation for the Thursday deadline and paper printing. Friday morning, we would all reconvene to talk about the publication.

From the look on Chris's face, I could tell he was amazed as well as impressed. He carefully ran his fingers across the colorful art splashed across the pages. "I can't believe this is like— over twenty years old?!"

"Or more," I painfully divulge.

"You guys basically had your own newspaper setup."

"Basically."

The rustling of pages stopped. Chris had found the story! He was done browsing and was ready to thoroughly examine the article. Stomping his foot on the floor, Chris shook the paper in an act of disbelief. Raising an eye to me, he yelled, "Ice-muthafuckin'-T!"

"Ice-muthafuckin'-T," I confirmed.

"Man, I gotta read this!"

"Well, that was the idea."

"I mean out loud!"

"Huh? No, no, no, that's not necessary. Chris, I know how—"

"Ice-muthafuckin'-T!" he repeated, oblivious to my response.

I admit, I was initially uncomfortable with the idea of having the story read to me, but once I knew Chris was adamant about doing it, I relaxed and actually started to feel a little warm and fuzzy inside. I was being tucked in and read one of my favorite bedtime stories—one I had written, no less! It doesn't get much better than that as a writer.

Chris began reading aloud. but I couldn't comprehend the meaning of his words because my mind was elsewhere, focused on a buried past being unearthed right before me. The bedtime story hadn't ushered me off into a blissful sleep; in fact, it had the opposite effect, bringing me out of a deep slumber by awakening feelings long dormant.

> • Rapper Ice T's song "Cop Killer" has raised the ire of police officers and politicians around the country. Yet, St. Petersburg police seem surprisingly protective of his freedom of speech.
>
> By Charles Smith
> PRESS STAFF
>
> Coming to a music store near you: Total recall.
>
> Local retailers are recoiling from controversial rapper Ice-T's song, *Cop Killer*, which glorifies the killing of police officers. Copies of the album, *Body Count*, have been yanked from the shelves of four South Florida record store chains. In Broward and Palm Beach counties, Record Bar, Record Town, Sound Warehouse and Camelot Music have all pulled the Time Warner release with no plans to sell it again. Nationwide, more than 1,000 stores have withdrawn *Body Count* from their collection of CDs and cassette tapes.
>
> City legislators, law enforcement agencies and religious organizations are combining to oppose sale of the album, and are urging people not to buy it where it is sold. The Chicago Police Department wrote to Time Warner demanding that the company remove the album from distribution. Alabama Gov. Guy Hunt, who is trying to have the album banned in his state, called for other governors to do the same.
>
> But these actions raise two questions: Is this an infringement of First Amendment rights? Will a ban prove effective?
>
> "If you cut freedom of expression today, what do you cut tomorrow?" asked St. Petersburg Police spokesman Wendell Creager. "I don't see how [legislators] could ban a song without infringing upon First Amendment rights. As an American citizen, [Ice-T] exercises his right to say what he wants; and I exercise my right not to purchase the record."
>
> Unlike officers in Chicago, St. Petersburg policeman Chuck Tatum does not feel the song will inspire violence against police officers. "It doesn't bother me, because I don't feel it influences a large majority of the nation," said Tatum. "There is enough violence on television. I think [Ice-T] took advantage of it as a marketing tool."
>
> Controversy sells. It's worked for artists such as Michael Jackson, Madonna and Prince. And apparently, it's working for Ice-T. Sam Goody in Fort Lauderdale is enjoying an increase in business due to the decision of other record stores to ban *Body Count*. "Recently, due to the controversy, it's hot as heck," said Dean Maffie, the store manager. "It's like when 2 Live Crew came out. Nobody bought [the band's album] until it was banned."
>
> "I'm never going to knock anyone's music," said St. Petersburg police officer Dave Crawford. "It's unfortunate, because he is stereotyping [police] the way he wouldn't want to be stereotyped as an African American. Two wrongs don't make a right."
>
> Information from the St. Petersburg Times and Chicago Tribune was used in this article.

I heard sounds: the keystrokes of anxious writers feverishly working against deadlines. The endless office murmurs between writers and copy editors discussing stories. The television broadcasts of sports highlights, the latest cross-town car chase, and other breaking news. I remembered the rush of coming in to work on Monday morning to find the most recent copy of the City Times sitting on my desk. I would turn to the sports section and see my byline. Prideful, I would slump back into my chair, knowing my story had been circulating around the city all weekend.

The writing bug had bitten me once again! Unfortunately, I wasn't able to enjoy my nostalgic trip to the past for long, as it was interrupted by more unintelligible words from Chris. Suddenly, I felt an arm on my shoulder.

"You all right, dude? I lost you for a minute. Where did you go?"

"Somewhere I hadn't been in a long time," I admitted, "and it was wonderful!"

"Uh …yeah, okay. What I was saying is I bet most cops didn't respond to the song the way these guys did in your story."

"No," I firmly stated. "Not at all. Especially in Los Angeles, where, at the time, the police and young black males seemed to have a love- hate relationship: loving to hate each other." Chris laughed at my wordplay, but with a hint of discomfort. "I couldn't even imagine being black and living in LA then with my temper. That verdict was a joke! I can't believe they let those fuckin' guys walk after watching that videotape!"

I huffed and shook my head as I remembered that verdict and the subsequent shit-storm that had followed. "Neither could the rioters!"

"And you were in the middle of all that shit?!"

"Ha!" I laughed at Chris's presumption. "I wasn't exactly in the middle. I mean, I wasn't busting out storefront windows and hurling bricks at innocent people driving down the street, but I was close enough to the outbreaks to where a few tanks were lined up along Manchester, which was a major street by my house. As a black man, though, I felt the pain, frustration, and anger of the people who were out there rioting and looting!"

"How did you cope with it?"

Chris had now switched pretend occupations to that of therapist after doing an admirable job at playing the role of journalist. I'd never really thought about how I had dealt with everything that was going on in my life during those turbulent times: riots breaking out, finals week, college graduation, being in love for the first time with my college sweetheart.

Then it came to me. "What helped me was I realized this was a pivotal time in my life and I had a choice to make," I said. "I knew in a little over a month, I was heading to Florida (the Poynter Institute), and so that is what I focused on."

"You were lucky," Chris observed.

"Blessed! But the Poynter was just the first step. The LA Times's answer to the chaos and violence that erupted in the inner cities due to the social unrest was the City Times. When I got back to LA, I almost immediately got a writing gig with the paper and thus was able to transition smoothly into the next phase of my life."

Chris retracted his prior statement then reassessed my situation. "I take that back; you weren't lucky—you were damn lucky!"

No argument on my part, only further clarification. "People in Los Angeles expressed their disapproval with what was going on in different ways," I said. "Ice-T's response was 'Cop Killer.'"

"There may be a 'Cop Killer' remix if things continue going the way they are going!"

"I seriously doubt it. It seems most rappers these days are more concerned with material things than social matters. If that's not true, their music certainly doesn't suggest otherwise."

"That's why you gotta respect a guy like Ice-T who would put out that kinda song!"

"Yes, sir. The true genius is that he reached a rock audience that wasn't really listening to rap—which made the song blow up even more."

"What's funny is now he plays a cop on television," Chris said. "I remember him talking about how ironically things had worked out. Have you seen his show?"

"You're talking about Law & Order: Special Victims Unit, right?"

"Yeah."

"A couple of episodes."

"Ice-T really is a P-I-M-P, man! Famous rapper. Famous actor. Famous father." Chris then pointed to a life-sized poster on the wall. "And he's married to Coco!"

I gazed at the picture of Ice-T's curvaceous wife. Her product line, Coco-licious, decorated the side wall. Play beads, a Love Bunny vibrator, a Slender 'G' vibrator, and an assortment of provocative lingerie were all strategically placed (thanks to yours truly) around her seductive likeness. "I hear you, Chris. It doesn't seem fair, does it?"

Chris tapped his finger against the newspaper and reminded me, "You'll always have this, though! You've done all right, too!"

"Yeah ... I suppose to some degree. But in retrospect, I think I respect Ice-T the most for being an inspiration to a twenty-one-year- old black male at the time with aspirations of educating and entertaining people with his words."

"If Ice-T knew that, I think he would be proud of what that guy has accomplished!"

"That guy is very appreciative of your kind words," I replied with a smile.

"You see—yet another reason Ice-T is a P-I-M-P!"

"A *true* P-I-M-P!"

Satiated for the moment, Chris tossed the paper on the counter and headed back to the cleaning closet. Passing by Coco's display, he took a final glance at her and muttered, "Ice muthafuckin'-T!"

That about summed it up for me, too. Ice-muthafuckin'-T!

Note:

During the writing of this book, Alton Sterling, Philandro Castile, Michael Brown, Freddie Gray, Sandra Bland, as well as many other people of color lost their lives in encounters with the police. Treyvon Martin was slain by an individual acting under the guise of a neighborhood watchman. Shortly after Sterling and Castile were killed, a lone gunman in Dallas took the lives of five officers in retaliation. This is the ultimate example of the dangers we all face in a society that operates daily under the practices of stereotyping, labeling, and judging.

Police brutality against any and all races, religions, and ethnicities is wrong ... as is any resulting retaliation against law enforcement. San Francisco quarterback Colin Kaepernick made headlines by kneeling during the national anthem in protest to this alarming trend. To those who risk their lives every day to protect and serve the community without bias and prejudice, I applaud you. Hopefully, your efforts can be the example used to reestablish trust in the communities between cops and civilians.

WALKING THE DOG

In everyday life, you'll find people taking their dogs along with them to malls, grocery stores, and other places of business. Why should the adult world be any different than the outside world? (I don't call it the real world because life behind these tinted doors is often more real.)

There is a customer who comes to the store and purchases *Buttman* magazines by the dozen. He's middle-aged and sports a long, wiry beard speckled with gray. From the looks of his outfits, his closet hasn't had a fashion update since 1979, but what distinguishes him most is his diminutive four-legged companion: a miniature Doberman Pinscher, or min-pin, whose scurrying legs become a black-and-tan blur while attempting to keep up with his long-striding steps.

As the customer walks around the display, she obediently follows, careful not to pass him and patiently sitting at his heels whenever he stops to browse. One day I asked, "So you get the magazine. ... What's in it for the pooch?"

Flipping pages, he laughed. "Believe me, she is well taken care of. She got one beef-cheddar treat before she came in and will get another when we get in the car—if she's good."

"From what I can see, she behaves better than 90 percent of my customers. What's the name of those treats?"

Another time, a gentleman came in with a Chihuahua, easily my least favorite dog. If the word "annoying" were accompanied by a visual in the dictionary, it would be of a Chihuahua barking and yapping! Paris Hilton didn't do me any favors, either, when she decided to popularize the dog as a fashion accessory.

To this customer's credit (and unlike the infamous socialite), he wasn't carrying the Chihuahua in a "doggie purse," but he did have it tucked between his arm and rib cage like a miniature football. The dog's feet never touched ground the entire time they were in the store. I once questioned his decision to tote the pup around instead of letting it use its legs for their intended purpose. His response: "I don't want her walking on this dirty carpet!"

Excuse me? I supposed the concrete outside that was stained with spilled beer and pigeon shit was much cleaner. I took offense. "Dirty? Sir, I'll have you know this carpet was just deep-cleaned last night." (The store is like my second home so, yes, I tend to get a tad sensitive.)

He found my comment to be about as funny as I found his response logical, and the way he treated his pet only furthered my disdain for these dogs, which have always appeared to me as nothing more than glorified rats.

Dogs are man's best friend, it is often said, but I met a woman who took her canine relationship to a whole other level.

It was 2013, a week before Memorial Day. A couple rushed through the door. The man grabbed the key off the counter and darted toward the bathroom. His female counterpart turned left, passed by me and went over to the fetish area.

Obviously, they had been here before.

She surveyed the wall, then grabbed a flogger and paddle off their respective hooks. With a hesitant glance from underneath her brimmed hat, she asked, "Do you allow dogs on the premises?"

Odd timing, I thought. Generally speaking, people ask that question before they come in-side the store. Perhaps, I reasoned, they were going to be a while and she had decided to go get the dog out of the car.

"Yes, they are allowed," I told her, "if the dog is on a leash or is small enough to be carried around."

"I have a leash for him, and he is completely trained and housebroken," she assured me.

"That sounds fine."

She came to the counter with a few items in hand. "I'd like to purchase these before I go get him."

The total came to $43.09. After completing the transaction, she thanked me and rushed off to find her companion.

I went back to my business of tagging videos and performing other miscellaneous tasks to help pass the day. About fifteen minutes later, a regular came to the counter looking for the bathroom key.

"Is someone in the restroom?" he asked.

"I don't think so," I replied. "The key is right …" Missing! It had been a while since I'd last seen that guy take it. I had just assumed that the couple had made their way to a booth. "I think there is someone in the bathroom, sir, but they should be out in a minute. If not, I will go knock on the door and see what's the holdup."

Muhammad would not have to go to the mountain, however, because the mountain came to Muhammad!

Strange, disturbing sounds began to emanate from the back of the store. Muffled grunts. Whimpering. A few throaty growls.

"Did you hear that?" I asked the guy.

"Yeah," he responded, puzzled. "What the fuck was it? Is there a dog in here?"

I shook my head. "I don't know. This lady gave me the impression she was bringing a dog into the store. I'm guessing her friend must have smuggled him in here without me noticing."

"How could you have missed it?" he wondered. "Sounds like a pretty big dog, but it must have a muzzle on or something."

The bathroom door flung open.

Out stepped the woman wearing a platinum-blonde wig, dressed in all black attire: a spike studded, vinyl/latex bra, leather chaps that circled and snapped at the waist, satin panties, and six-inch platform heels. A remote control was in her right hand, and in her left, a leash still attached to something in the bathroom

The regular and I gazed upon this remarkable transformation in astonishment, our mouths agape. "Holy shit!" he belted out. "How do I get a job at this place?"

"Holy shit," I blurted. "How did I ever get involved with this place?"

The store hallway became the woman's Fashion Week catwalk as she strutted her 6'1" frame toward the front of the store. Each customer she passed along the way became an eager photographer, frantically pulling out a cell phone to snap a picture.

We were all standing at attention (pun intended), transfixed by this astonishing sight. Next came the obvious question: What the hell was at the end of that long leash? Again, Moses had no need to worry.

Once she reached the front of the store, she barked out, "Come!" As commanded, her approximately 6'2", 225-pound "pet" lumbered out of the bathroom and down the hallway on all fours. A black leather dog hood covered its head. Skin-tight black boxer briefs covered "everything else." The hood apparatus included a mask that blocked his vision, so to successfully navigate around the store, the pet had to follow the tug of the leash.

Despite being in shock, the regular poignantly captured the moment once again. "Holy fuck! What is going on around here?"

I tapped him on the shoulder. "If you're still interested in a job, you can have mine!"

The woman was pleased with her dog's behavior. "Good boy!" she praised. "Mommy likes it when you listen."

"So when he's disobedient, is it the flog or paddle?" I asked, remembering her purchases.

"Neither—that is what this is for." She raised her hand, showing me the remote control. "He's usually a good boy, but when he is bad, all I have to do is press this button. Would you like a demonstration?"

"I would," the regular shouted enthusiastically.

Who let Conan the Barbarian in the building? I wondered. "We don't condone animal cruelty at this establishment," I said, cracking a half-smile. As if being half-naked, led around by a leash, crawling on the floor at a porn shop with other grown men looking on wasn't abuse enough.

"Oh, it's okay!" she said, trying to convince me. "I don't like to discipline him, but he loves it!"

The button was pressed and met with immediate results. A few violent headshakes were followed by a garbled yelp that could be heard through the hood. Almost instinctively, the dog went into a prone position, bowing at his master's perfectly pedicured feet.

"That was awesome," Conan gushed. "Do it again!"

Easy there, Conan! I could use one of those gadgets for you right about now! "That's quite effective," I admitted, "but not necessary. I don't want to have to alert the Humane Society."

"But it is necessary," she corrected me. "He's just a filthy animal who deserves to be *punished!*"

He was just a good boy a minute ago, wasn't he?! I thought. That was when I realized their role playing was all about humiliation—his. And much to his delight!

Conan struck again. "What kind of tricks can he do?"

"I think we've seen enough," I intervened. I'd had my fill of male- dog impersonators. Not to mention, a not-so-small crowd was beginning to gather. Unfortunately, my opinion was of the minority, as muttering voices started to chant, "More."

The master saw this as an opportunity to display her dominance. "Roll over," she commanded. Her pet did so. I didn't bother telling either of them the floor hadn't been cleaned in two weeks.

"Play dead." Again, he did as he was told. "I'll bet you're thirsty, baby. Mommy is going to get you some water." He growled and then barked. She grabbed a cup off the top of the water cooler and filled it halfway. The pet was now on his hands and knees. She unzipped the part of the mask that covered his mouth and placed the cup in front of him. He bowed down and licked water out of the cup, just like a dog!

Conan screamed, "Fuckin' awesome!"

At that moment, I had another revelation—this one about Conan: He wasn't barbaric—he was *envious*, wanting to be on the end of that leash!

"I saw a video on YouTube where this woman got her dog to eat her out by putting peanut butter on her pussy!" a customer shouted. "Does your dog eat pussy?"

"Oh, very well!" the woman replied. "Pussy is one of his favorite treats!"

"But sadly, one he won't be partaking of now!" I regretfully informed the amorous mob.

The natives were getting raunchier than usual, and I had to restore some semblance of order. "The dog park is closed for today, everybody!" The patrons grunt and groan. "However, I'm sure for all interested, the owner probably wouldn't mind *training* a few of you animals!"

This was music to her ears. "Ooh—I would love to break in a *new* pet!" Conan smiled.

She walked her dog back to the bathroom, and the crowd began to disperse. Some left, and others found refuge in booths. Finally able to remove my zookeeper hat, I sat down to process what had just taken place.

"Never a dull moment, eh?" a guy remarked. I exhaled. "They are few and far between."

The couple, now both fully dressed, came up and thanked me for my open-mindedness. "Oh honey, I forgot something in the bathroom," the woman told her partner/pet. "Wait here—and be a good boy!"

Calmly and seemingly oblivious to the fact that he had just been crawling around the store on all fours, he asked, "So how is your day going?" now fully erect (standing, that is).

With a look of bewilderment, I responded, "Just another day in the life," then repeated, "just another day in the life!"

Suddenly, I heard a voice from the back command, "Come, boy!

Mommy is going to introduce you to her other pets." Is there a fuckin' kennel back there?! I wondered.

The woman reappeared, walking toward us with her newest pet—*Conan!* Collared and leashed, he crawled behind his new master, who was giddy with excitement. "Boys, we are going home. ... Mommy has new toys to try out!"

BEHIND CLOSED DOORS

The booth: A world unto itself. If those walls could talk, a New York Times bestselling novel could be the result! (Hmm.) It's a place where an individual's true nature is revealed. No wife. No boss. No bills. No filters. No facades. Think of the porn shop as a fallout shelter and the booths as underground private rooms where people can be safe in their secrecy from the public.

This anonymity is what makes the booths so popular. It allows for exploration, indulgence, or simple relaxation, the common thread among the occupants being that they can leave behind the life they know to experience something new and different, if they so choose— which they usually do!

The booths can also be a very scary place—for clerks!—as evidenced by a story Bart shared with me one morning about Eric (a customer who gets on all of our collective nerves).

Bart and I get along well, one of the reasons being that our temperaments are very similar.

We're both laid back, sarcastic, and love to joke around, so it is not uncommon for one of us to start laughing in the middle of the other's story because we know where it's going.

Before Bart began his narration, he prefaced it with "I don't know what this fool was thinking …" Usually when he starts a story with these words, it's a good one!

"So, I'm walking around the back, sweeping the booths. All's pretty quiet—too quiet, if you know what I mean?"

I knew all too well. It's like the calm before the storm. You can sense it, feel it in the air. Something wicked this way comes!

"I didn't think anyone else was in the store ... and then I heard someone moving around in Booth 4." Bart got into character as he told the story, looking confused and carefully scanning the room, reenacting the moment. "The booth light was off (no money in the meter) and the door was cracked, so I gently pushed it open." Bart's right hand slowly moved forward, mimicking the act.

A clerk is wise to proceed with caution in these situations. For one, if there is a person in the booth, this serves as a warning to them that someone is coming in. It also saves unwitting employees from potentially traumatic experiences! Most of the time it works, but other times ...

"There was Eric!" Bart recalled. Even in the retelling of the story, he was becoming flustered. "His left hand cuffed to the ceiling, pants down around his ankles! I was like, 'Dude, what the fuck are you doing?! Quit dangling from the ceiling and put your damn pants on!'"

"Dangling, huh?"

"Twig and berries!"

"Sorry I asked."

"Yeah, man! I was pissed! I didn't want to see that shit! You could tell he was embarrassed, too!"

"Why hadn't he just uncuffed himself?"

"Because apparently, the key was in his pants pocket—which he couldn't reach with his free hand."

"I'm sure he was able to reach something else." "Aw man, I don't even want to think about that!"

According to Bart, Eric told him he had been handcuffed by a companion who had told him to "hang tight" until he returned. Supposedly, that exchange had taken place ten minutes before Bart arrived.

"So I asked him how long he was going to hang there without calling for help," Bart said. "He probably would have still been there if it weren't for me."

"Christopher Columbus you were not, Bart."

"What do you mean?"

"The natives had already discovered that territory; they just weren't interested in cultivating the land."

Bart paused momentarily. "No wonder he wasn't calling for help."

"Bingo! So how did he get down? You lend him a helping hand?"

"Very funny! But, yeah, I had to! I couldn't just let him hang there until he was ripe! So I put a pair of gloves on, got the keys, and took the cuff off."

"Aw, that's very sweet of you."

"Then I told him he needed to find another way to occupy his time for a few weeks because I had seen enough of him."

"In more ways than one."

"You got that shit right! And don't you know, the dude tried to come the next day—three times!"

"Cock crowing."

"These fuckers are on divine time, man. One year to them is like a few weeks. A lifetime ban may keep them away for a few months—if that!"

It was now my turn to share, but before I could regale my colleague with one of my own astonishing tales of tail, I was halted by a young Asian girl seeking a vibe that was "sparkly."

"Is this a good one?" she questioned. "I've never done this before, and there are so many!"

"Not to worry," I comforted her. "It can be a bit intimidating for a first-timer. This is a popular brand. I'll put some batteries in and you can see how it works."

"Oh my God!" Her voice squeaked. "Right here?"

"Where would you suggest? You don't want to get home and it not work. We don't do ex-changes."

"Oh my God! I would never bring it back!"

"That's what they all say."

I roughly pulled the latex glove over my fingers and quickly released it, causing it to pop against the palm of my hand.

"And what exactly are those for?" she sheepishly inquired.

"Surgery—I'm going in!"

"OH MY GOD!" she squealed. "This is so embarrassing!"

"Doctor Dré ... I have faith that you can handle this procedure without my assistance," Bart confided. "Therefore, I will be relieving myself, temporarily."

"Very well."

"You guys are funny!" the girl giggled.

The operation was a success! I placed the toy in front of her and warned, "That dial on the bottom adjusts the speed, so don't turn it too quickly." Of course, she did just that, lacking the slow, steady hand (as do most novices) necessary to operate a vibrator with escalating speeds. Eagerness getting the best of her, she turned the cap too fast and the vibrator became a wild flounder in her hand. "Oh my God!" she shrieked, tossing her catch back onto the boat. It rattled and flailed about on the counter. "Do something!" she insisted.

I grabbed a pen, pretending to stab at the squirmy device (it came pre-lubed). "This isn't working. ... I need a net!"

She laughed hysterically while reaching out and firmly grabbing her prize with both hands. She used a gentler twist of the wrist this time, and the fish went lifeless. "Oh my God! That was too funny!"

"See, that wasn't so bad. You showed it who's boss!"

"I have to learn to control the speeds, or else I might hurt something down there!"

"Yeah, be nice to your clit!"

"Oh my God! You are too much!" She snatched up her black bag and waved as she left the docks. "Thanks. You have a wonderful day!" she called, and then she was gone fishing.

A few minutes later, Bart returned. "I cleaned up a little bit while I was in the back. Swept the booths and gave the floor a once-over with the mop."

"Cool."

"So let's hear what you got."

"Well, my story doesn't take place in the booths, but it does demonstrate the power that the booth has as a ..."

"Aphrodisiac," Bart offers.

"More like a hormone-inciter!"

"Fair enough."

I told Bart that a couple had come came in one day around noon. The female was a haggard-looking blonde well past her prime but quite possibly a high-school cheerleader at one time (long, long ago ... in a decade far, far away!). Her companion was a short, stocky His- panic male in a white wife-beater. Tattoos signifying his gang affiliation were emblazoned across his chest, along with two tears (each representing a life he had taken) on his cheek.

I watched on camera as they walked to the back before she directed him to a booth. They entered but didn't stay in there for very long, perhaps five to ten minutes. Apparently, that was more than enough time to get the desired effect. They then came up front and she grabbed a handful of condoms and eagerly rushed to the counter while he went outside to wait for her.

"I've been waiting for this!" she said.

Feigning ignorance, I asked, "What might that be?"

"My friend just got out (of prison) and hasn't had sex in years!"

With a woman, that is!

"All that penned-up frustration. ... Can you imagine how he is going to fuck me?"

Yup, like you're a man! She paid for the prophylactics and scurried out the door. Somewhere out there, this couples' reenactment of a sex scene from *American Me* was set to begin.

About thirty minutes went by, and it was time for my break. When the relief clerk arrived, I decided to go to the bar a few blocks down the street to get a chicken Philly cheesesteak. When I got there, the place was packed! It was karaoke night.

"Did you see George?" Bart asked. "He's really cool ... makes good drinks too!"

"Yeah, as a matter of fact, he took my order. I had to go to the restroom, and there was a long line for the customers, so he gave me the key to the employee bathroom."

"Like I said, he is a cool guy."

"Yeah, but I probably would have been better off going to the customer bathroom."

"Why?"

"Well ... as I'm turning the door handle, I hear unusual yet all too familiar noises."

"Like ..."

"Like flesh smacking and the sound of something creaking like it's being pulled from a wall!"

"What the fuck?"

"*Fuck* is right! I crack the door open and I hear, 'That's it, baby. ... Fuck me like this is your last night of freedom!' followed by, 'You like that big dick, don't you, *gringa*?! I'm going to turn you around and put it in your *culo!*'"

"Oh shit! Are you serious? A couple were in their fuckin'!"

"No, *the couple*—the cheerleader and her ex-con! I peeked in, and the first thing I see is the artwork splattered across this guy's back: numbers and symbols. More gang affiliations, I'm sure."

"What were they *doin'* in there?"

"Each other!" And quite well, might I add! Bodies were contorted in compromising positions, limbs everywhere: him behind her, her left hand against the sink, his right hand cupping her ass. Her left leg draped over his left leg, which rested on the toilet, his left hand clutching a handful of bleached-blonde hair, her right hand reaching around and squeezing his right cheek, his right leg firmly planted on the ground, bracing them both.

Bart scratched his thick beard in disbelief. "Fuck, dude!"

"Yeah, I turned right around and promptly took the key back to George. I told him the bathroom was occupied. He told me it shouldn't be and asked who was in there, and I told him about the ongoing game of naked Twister!"

"What did he say?"

"He said that it was their new bartender, Becky, and he would talk to her about having sex in the bathroom with her 'boyfriends' on her break!"

"That's crazy!"

"That's the power of the booth!"

THINK TANK

Sifting and sorting through one's personal baggage can be messy; however, I believe it to be necessary for spiritual growth, in addition to being mentally therapeutic. When business is slow, the shop is a surprisingly perfect place for meditation. During those quiet times—the intermittent silence between oohs, aahs, and "yes-daddy-fuck-me-like-the-whore-I-am" screams—there are opportunities for much-needed reflection and reassessment of my own value system.

I ponder this concept of good and bad, and how society at large uses it to define our customers—and the idea of sex in general. I've come to understand the association of good and bad with types of behavior to be a subjective practice that can be very detrimental to a relationship in its application.

My involvement with Miryam, my first real girlfriend, was proof of this. She was my college sweetheart: well-bred, private-school educated, a product of old money. From her impeccable flair for fashion and accessories to her engaging personality and radiant smile, everything about Miryam's outward appearance oozed *perfection*.

What I learned was that we sometimes dress up the outside to mask the ugliness we feel inside. Miryam would say, "Always present yourself as if everything is wonderful!" She had become such a master of this disguise technique that even I was fooled.

Like all of us, Miryam had her issues. One that plagued the better part of our seven-year relationship was her internal struggle with how a *good* girl should conduct herself. Miryam's opinions were heavily swayed by her Middle Eastern culture—which emphasizes sexual piety among its women—and an ultraconservative upbringing (Republican and Catholic). All of this made for a perfect storm of sexual confusion for a twenty-one-year-old virgin experiencing love and lust for the first time.

Before we'd actually had intercourse—more than a year into our relationship—we experimented. I remember her once saying to me, "Anything that feels this good has to be wrong!" Unfortunately, our relationship would come to be defined by these words. In her eyes, it was okay to do certain things to make each other feel good if they didn't make us feel *too good*—because that would be wrong.

Looking back, I realize how powerful—and unfortunate—a statement like that is, simply because there are teenagers and young adults today who are afraid, ashamed, or uncertain about their sexuality because society has used negative associations instead of education as a means of abstinence and birth control.

I believe this all starts when we are young, when others—usually parents—create our codes of conduct, which are generally based off their own feelings and experiences. As we grow older, we begin to develop our own belief systems apart from, and sometimes skeptical of, the ones taught to us. This human programming glitch known as puberty is when we start to question the things taught to us and begin to think more independently.

Commands given by parents and other influential adults in our lives—particularly concerning those things of a sexual nature— are slowly met with curiosity, and as we move from adolescence into adulthood, we begin to develop our own sexual tastes—and hopefully realize what may be "bad" or "wrong" for one person might be "good" or "right" for another, leaving a significantly large gray area.

I'm of the opinion that the only "black and white" that exists in terms of defining acceptable behavior is "legal and illegal." These are the absolutes—and sometimes even that line gets blurred.

Some customers have said they were embarrassed to be seen in a porn shop or shouldn't be in a "place like this." I ask why. Everyone and everything that can has sex. Isn't that how we got here? How the planet is repopulated? How bloodlines and legacies are passed down? Religious beliefs aside, procreation—the simple yet universal act that allows mankind to exist through the generations—is why we are all here, right?

Man needs air, food, water, and shelter to ensure survival, but his sex drive could possibly be his greatest urge. Even in the animal kingdom, many males risk their lives to reproduce with females and continue the circle of life. I've seen countless documentaries showing lions, sea lions, seals, hippopotamus, rams, and even spiders fighting and dying just for the right to mate.

There is also research indicating that many animals other than humans engage in sexual activity even when conception is not a possible outcome.[3] Some studies, such as those done on one of our closest relatives, the bonobo, shows that sex aids in solidifying bonds and supporting the social structure of their society.[4] Could this also hold true for humans, the "most highly evolved" animal? And if so, why is the deed so unnecessarily yoked by guilt, shame, rules, regulations, and hang-ups? Just as animals are drawn to have sex for the purposes of procreation *and* pleasure, so are people!

---

[3] "Do Animals Have Sex for Pleasure," Jason G. Goldman, 13 June 2014, http://www.bbc.com/future/story/20140613-do-animals-have-sex-for-fun.
[4] "Yes, Other Animals Do Have Sex for Fun," Jamie Lawson, Durham University, 3 August 2015, http://blogs.discovermagazine.com/crux/2015/08/03/animal-sex/#.V56tDo4mmWY.

On more than one occasion, customers have felt the need to tell me it's their first time visiting a porn shop. They'll say things like "I don't usually come to places like this" or "This toy isn't for me—it's for my *friend!*" What they don't realize is *I don't care!* But I *understand* having struggled with similar feelings when I started working at the store. You are operating from fear—fear of judgment from yourself and others based on what you have read, heard, and seen on television, in church, at school, and at home from family, friends, or acquaintances.

Therein lies the problem.

Western society has taught us to have a rather distorted image of what is "acceptable" or "normal" in terms of sexual behavior. This is a fact that dates back to Victorian times, when sex was seen as something to be "endured" by the wife because sexual desire was experienced only by males.[5] When a woman did express sexual desire, it was considered a disease that needed to be eradicated immediately with drastic measures such as removing the sex organs.

The Victorians believed that sex and sexual desire weren't something experienced by well-bred, upper-class people; only men and women (like prostitutes) of lower class and inferior breeding engaged in such activities—which meant sex and everything related to it were shameful and should be hidden. Perhaps such distorted beliefs are what spawned porn shops, which provided a safe place to express and explore one's sexual desires that are looked upon as taboo.

---

[5] "The Victorian Era," History of Human Sexuality in Western Culture, Gabriella Pastor, Chelsea Mageland, Sara Findley, March 4, 2011, http://historyofsexuality.umwblogs.org/pre-20th-century/victorian-era-2/.

I notice how the self-righteous deem themselves worthy to pass judgment on businesses like this and its patrons—over the years, many a bible-toting, born-again Christian has ducked inside the shop to foretell of our impending doom!—but I have witnessed some of the most vocal opponents of sex and sex establishments (politicians, pastors, televangelists) being brought down by the very same behaviors they decry. It seems because they have the so-called decency to do the same things, but in a private manner, they believe they are qualified to come down on those who partake of these same activities in public establishments. Though I may not condone everything I see—or hear, for that matter—I certainly cannot condemn anyone else for partaking in safe, consensual sexual activity— particularly with one's self (masturbation.)

And about masturbation, why is it that when women do it, society views it as sexy but when men indulge in self-gratification, it's largely portrayed as a disgusting act? I know women get the short end of the stick in regards to more socially relevant double standards, but does this one have to have such a glaring discrepancy in imagery?

Female masturbation is widely viewed as a beautiful experience. A typical cinematic portrayal would find an attractive, scantily clad woman with gentle curves lying in her bed. The room is dimly lit by a moon peeking through the window. Soft music plays as the circular movement under the covers steadily quickens until, finally, her writhing body and pleasure-filled moans crescendo into a mind-blowing orgasm.

This is a stark contrast to the seedy motel room where we find a middle-aged man lying belly up on his bed, his stomach ballooning out from underneath a dingy wife-beater, his scruffy salt-and-pepper beard badly in need of grooming. On the nightstand, a dirty glass ashtray is littered with several mashed cigarette butts. Blue light from the television illuminates the room a la *Poltergeist*. His right hand holds the remote while the left works his other instrument, his "cum face" ugly enough to make the lesbian say to the hetero, "Now do you get it?"

Slight exaggeration? Possibly. But the greater element of shame attached to men caught in the act is undeniable. Pee-wee Herman and George Michael were vilified—and arguably, rightfully so—for masturbating in public. But if they were two beautiful females, would there have been such public outrage?

Our store sells several toys, including small bullets, eggs, and other vibrators that are designed to conveniently fit in purses and small handbags. The reason is simple: orgasms on the go. I've dated women who have shared stories about "rubbing one out" in their car (Mallory while *driving*), at their desk at work, or in the employee bathroom. Instead of public consternation, they probably would attract an eager audience.

Here at the store, however, many male customers duck in and out because they don't want others to know about their secret fantasies for fear of being ridiculed. I tell them women have their pornography too—it's called romance novels! I once told an intrigued customer, "Men need pictures, women don't! Their minds work differently. Give them a concept and their imagination can create an image more powerful than any photograph or picture. But men need that *visual!*" The once quizzical look on the man's face was wiped away by new found wisdom. "Show me the honey!" he shouted.

"Exactly," I responded.

The man claimed he suffered from the Madonna-whore complex[6] and masturbation helped him deal with it. "I place my wife on a pedestal and could never see myself doing naughty things with the mother of my children." So, he came to the shop to release—literally and figuratively—while watching couples engaged in sexual acts he couldn't imagine doing with his wife.

Just as I did as a kid, most boys fantasize about girls. They have wet dreams when they are asleep and masturbate when they are awake. Is a boy supposed to suddenly mature and stop just because he grows older? Of course not. In fact, his sexual thoughts will be even more in-depth and detailed. The difference is, a boy may foolishly act upon his fantasies without thinking, whereas a man will fantasize but (should) think before acting.

"Masturbating helps keep me honest," another gentleman told me one day. "It keeps me from cheating on my wife because I can have any woman (on the DVDs) I see. How many men get that in real life?" Which brings me to another observation about gender distinctions that has been reinforced during my time at the store, this one about relationships: A woman will usually seek out one man to fulfill all her needs, but a man (generally) will find many women (real or imagined) to satisfy his *one* need.

"Coming here allows me to indulge and then go home to my wife guilt-free," the gentleman continued.

---

[6] This psychological complex is said to develop in men who see women as either saintly Madonnas or debased prostitutes. Men with this complex desire a sexual partner who has been degraded (the whore) while they cannot desire the respected partner (the Madonna). "Sigmund Freud and His Impact on Our Understanding of Male Sexual Dysfunction," Uwe Harmann, 2009, The Journal of Sexual Medicine 6 (8): 2332-2339. doi:10.1111/j.1743- 6109.2009.01332.x.

"Does she know you come here?" I followed up.

Shaking his head adamantly, he said, "Hell no! She would kill me! The first thing she would say is, 'What ... I'm not enough?!'" That's a topic for another day.

"SPILL IN BOOTH 2!"

Every year, Americans must deal with the devastating effects of natural disasters. Hurricanes slam the Southeast. Tornadoes shred the Midwest. Earthquakes shake the West Coast. We experienced our own type of "natural disaster" at Video Expo one day, thanks to a rather excitable customer. She came in the store accompanied by a familiar face. Mack, as he called himself, was short, stocky, and built like an upright pit bull. He was known for his badass demeanor—and his fetish for dressing up in women's lingerie.

A study in contradiction, Mack would be labeled in society as a homo-thug: masculine in the streets and feminine in the sheets. Mack's female friend was not at all happy about his unwillingness to share a particular accessory in her time of need—a direct violation of the girl code. "He has forty-five wigs. You would think he could lone me *one*," she complained while eyeballing the mannequin. "Can I have this, sir? I need a wig for my job interview and *this* would be perfect."

"*Have*, no! *Buy, yes!*"

"Can you discount the price?"

"No, sorry."

"You wouldn't happen to have one lying around back there somewhere, would you?"

We do have a lost-and-found department. (It's a plastic fishbowl originally used for holding packets of lube.) Items inside vary from cell phones to sunglasses to expired driver's licenses and credit cards. But no wigs. Wait a minute ... there was something. I remembered an old hairpiece that I had taken off one of the mannequins a while back.

One of the customers had thought it would be cute to crayon a red streak down a few of the long platinum-blonde strands. He called it highlighting. My boss called it vandalism and banned the guy from the store. Anyway, I had put the wig (along with some ripped lingerie) inside a black bag and tossed it in a sliding drawer, somewhere. Ah, there it was! Luckily for her, I hadn't gotten around to throwing it out.

"Oh my God, I love it!" she squeaked—a reaction to be expected based on her appearance.

She looked every bit the little girl who couldn't wait to sneak into Mommy's closet to play dress-up. Her makeup looked as if it had been applied in the dark. She wore a faded purple cardigan sweater, ripped black fishnet stockings, and bone-white high heels, badly scuffed.

And now, thanks to me, the ensemble was completed by a platinum-blonde wig—with crayon highlights.

One man's trash is another woman's treasure—a woman currently skipping off to the bathroom in fashion delight. At times, I love my job simply because the little things truly make my people happy.

And about little things, "Can I get a small bottle of video head cleaner?" a customer requested, walking up. The voice belonged to David, a regular and a self-proclaimed former rock star (hard to believe) whose career had allegedly flamed out because of excessive drug use (not so hard to believe.) Half the time I saw David, he was intoxicated; the other half, he was a drink or snort away—but every time I saw him, he had a story to tell.

Today was no different. His dissertation would be on how production of crystal methamphetamine had changed over the years. David gazed at me through half-bloodshot eyes, teetering from side to side. He was trying but failing to stand still. "Being a Chicagoan, I admit that's a pretty good impersonation of the Sears Tower on a windy day," I mocked, referring to his swaying motion. "Which historic monument will you imitate next?"

"Dude, you can't make jokes, because I will lose my focus. I'm having a difficult time as it is standing up straight."

"Got it! Leaning Tower of Pisa?"

He hiccupped a few laughs, his sense of humor somewhat dulled by the effects of alcohol. "Okay, I'm going to begin."

"All right."

"Back in the day, I used to do every drug possible *except* heroin and cocaine," David recollected. "Now my only battle is with alcohol. Back then, crystal meth was pure. The main ingredient was ephedrine and there were no other extra additives. I knew what I was putting into my body—you can't say that these days."

What had gotten David started on this subject was the sight of a few meth heads roaming around outside. On their "best behavior," crystal-meth addicts speak quickly in incoherent run-on sentences with no real point. They are antsy and constantly moving one body part or another, appearing uncomfortable in their own skins. At their worst, they endlessly wander about, wide-eyed, twitching nervously and talking to themselves.

"Today, people mix meth with synthetics like Drano, brake fluid, lighter fluid, sodium hydroxide …" David enumerated. The more he rattled off the toxins on his checklist, the easier it was for me to understand the odd and disturbing behavior of meth heads. "Sometimes they add anhydrous ammonia, iodine, and even hydrochloric acid."

The physical toll exacted on the body by these poisons is blatantly obvious: drastic weight loss, glossy eyes, sunken-in cheeks, acne-ridden faces. Open sores aren't uncommon, either, as addicts often pick at their bumps with fingernails or other sharp objects.

"My girlfriend used to try to dig out her zits with a razor blade," Angelina (a coworker) once shared with me. Angelina was a former addict who hadn't used in more than a decade. "The worst part to me is the smell. Addicts have a certain smell seeping through their pores because of all the different chemicals they ingest—and other addicts can smell it!"

In my opinion, the worst part is if—and when—an addict ever quits, they spend the rest of their life resisting the temptation for one of the most highly addictive street drugs. "I don't fight the urge so much anymore," Angelina acknowledged at the time, "but if I get stressed, the urge shows up. I've been clean and sober for over twelve years—and I will die an addict."

Crystal meth is widely regarded as a party drug, much like cocaine was during the early eighties, but it quickly went from a drug of recreation to a drug of wreck-creation—as did cocaine. Highly potent, crystal meth first acts as a stimulant, but eventually, it begins to systematically destroy the body. Serious health conditions, including memory loss, aggression, psychotic behavior, and potential heart and brain damage, can occur.

Highly addictive, meth burns up the body's resources, creating a devastating dependence that can be relieved only by taking more of the drug. Crystal meth's effect is highly concentrated, and many users report getting addicted from the first time they use it.[7]

Crystal meth has long been the drug of choice in San Diego. "It's popular among the trailer parks because you can get it relatively cheap thanks to all the mix-ins," David said. At one time, San Diego held the dubious distinction of being the "meth capital of the United States."[8] David continued. "There are quite a few areas littered with trailer parks, so just do the math."

At the moment, however, the only number David was concerned with was $11.87—the cost of the head cleaner. Once he paid for the item, his instruction ended and his indulgence was set to begin. Off to a booth he wobbled.

Roughly thirty minutes of me selling DVDs and rearranging lubes later, Mack surfaced from the back and headed for the door—Imagine Tootsie meets Bozo the Clown!—but there was nothing comical about Mack's words of caution: "You got a situation back there I hope you are ready for!"

Great, now what?

I looked on the camera and saw his friend handing the mop to the janitor. Still wearing her wig, she bypassed her booth and came up to the front. "I told the janitor I cleaned up as much as possible—I did something in there."

---

[7] *The Truth About Crystal Meth*, Foundation For A Drug-Free World, 2006-2016, http://www.drugfreeworld.org/drugfacts/crystalmeth.html
[8] "California Southern District Drug Threat Assessment," National Drug Intelligence Center, December 2000 updated May 2002, https://www.justice.gov/archive/ndic/pubs/654/654t.htm

Oh Lord! I thought, the sentiment obviously written all over my face.

"No, nothing like that!" she quickly reassured me.

I didn't need—nor did I want—to know what had happened, so I simply thanked her for her efforts. But of course, she couldn't leave well enough alone. She leaned toward me with a look of embarrassment. "I squirted all over the bench and floor!" she disclosed. "I got it so wet that the guy couldn't really sit down!"

Time for damage assessment. "So, (Hurricane) Katrina, how many broken levies?" Laughing, she replied, "You're funny. Umm, I'd say two."

I'd say that was a rather modest number, seeing as the janitor was still feverishly mopping the floor. I thanked her once more before she left, and she redirected the gratitude. "No, thank *you* so much, sir! You have made my day! First with the wig, and then with the orgasms."

If only all natural disasters could have such happy endings.

BOYS WILL BE ... GIRLS

Customers always amaze me in regards to the amount of access they grant clerks into their personal lives. No comfortable reclining couch is necessary. No closed door quickly locked behind for privacy. No repeat weekly sessions to probe and uproot deep-seated problems and issues.

After just a simple hello, sometimes within minutes, I'm showered with details about individuals' deepest, darkest secrets—information they wouldn't dare divulge to friends, family, or even spouses.

I don't think the country's foremost psychologists and greatest psychiatric minds can lay stake to that claim, which is less a testament to my own abilities than to the powerfully disarming nature of the environment of the store.

Swinging open the tinted door is like cracking open a tooth: The nerve is fully exposed.

Covered-up indiscretions are laid bare. All the pain is right there for me to see. And though the stories vary, the story-tellers share a commonality: the cathartic effect they all experience after sharing.

It would be disingenuous of me to say it didn't take some time to get used to hearing these open and honest revelations, but once I did, the storytelling proved to be a mutually beneficial opportunity. Customers could exhale, feeling a burden had been lifted, and I learned to "breathe in" greater levels of tolerance and acceptance.

One such example was a three-way (conversation, that is) I had with Isaac and Sapphire. It was around this time that I began to entertain the idea of writing a book because it was becoming apparent I would need to do some sharing of my own one day.

Standing 6'4" in a pair of stiletto-heeled snakeskin platforms, Sapphire was a tall drink of transsexual, his sinewy frame wrapped in a Glam mini dress and long legs covered in thigh-high fence-net stockings.

"I'm a provocateur," he explained. "Some people will see me walking down the street and say, 'Look at that fag'; others may say, 'You go girl!' But I *will* provoke a reaction!"

I had always heard (and thought) that the shoes made the outfit, but according to Sapphire, I was wrong. "Honey, it's all about the attitude. It doesn't matter if I am wearing a dress with heels, or a baby tee with flip-flops, I rock *both* the same. Clothes don't wear me—I wear the clothes."

Merriam-Webster defines a transsexual as a person who psychologically identifies with the opposite sex- it is often said sex is a matter of the body, while gender occurs in the mind-and may seek to live as a member of this sex especially by undergoing surgery and hormone therapy to obtain the necessary physical appearance (as by changing the external sex organs).

For a male, this process involves the taking of female hormones and can include the option for surgery on the penis to replicate a vagina. One who chooses this drastic measure is known as a post-op, or a post-operational transsexual. One who has not yet decided to or will not go through this operation is referred to as pre-op, or preoperational.

The notion that being gay is a sign of sexual confusion is still a prevalent one today. Transsexuality pro-vides the perfect example for this school of thought, but Sapphire— real name Steven—argues that the transsexual lifestyle provides the best of both the masculine and feminine worlds. "There is no confusion on my part," Sapphire states matter-of-factly. "Sometimes I wake up and feel like being Steven, so I put on a pair of jeans and a shirt—and I'm *good*. Other times, I feel like going out and 'stomping around town,' so I get an outfit together, put on my makeup, and let *Sapphire* loose."

Isaac, a very "exotic-looking" gaymale (thanks to his half-black, half-Filipino heritage), had been quietly standing by through this conversation. Now, gazing into his compact, admiring the reflection, he cooed, "*Perfect*—nothing needs to be done here."

Sapphire, however, was less impressed. "Honey, it is so true when they say beauty is in the eye of the *beholder!*"

"Bitch, please!" Isaac sassed with a neck roll and semicircular finger snap. "You *wish* you looked like this!"

Sapphire tilted his head, similar to a canine when it hears a strange noise. (If he'd had long enough ears, they would have pointed skyward.) Surprised, he mumbled a comment through twisted lips. "Look ... I am tall, tantalizing, *and* too much for you or any man!" Pointing a rigid forefinger at Isaac, Sapphire added, "Don't *even* get me started!"

Now this had all the makings of a good catfight—nastiness, attitude, and humor—but I don't know if it qualifies as a catfight when the warring factions involve two men—even when they are *acting* like women.

I figured since they were attempting to portray the "gentler sex," I would encourage them to mimic more refined behavior. "Come now, ladies. Let's retract our claws and display a bit of civility towards one another on this fine Friday afternoon."

Isaac wasn't having it. "Girl, what you see is *au naturale*. God made *this* ... no artificial sweeteners here!"

Sapphire, not to be outdone, replied, "Honey, it doesn't matter if I take hormones. I am softer, smoother, and sexier. And I still got what God gave me, too—*right here!*"

I had done about as good a job at peacemaker as Rodney King had back in 1992; nobody was getting along. Just then, a customer approached the counter. Never had I been so happy to see an unfamiliar face.

"Excuse me, sir," he said, addressing me, "can you recommend a good solution to go along with this anal douche?"

Thank you! I could have simply suggested warm water, but here was my opportunity to go out onto the floor and escape this episode of cat-scratch fever.

Unfortunately, Sapphire ruined my plan. "The best thing is warm water," he piped up. "I just used one the other day, and that is what works best, in *my* opinion."

I had been foiled by another fast thinker—in hooker heels, no less—but I prided myself on being the quickest on the mental draw around these parts, so I would not be outwitted.

Wait ... that was it! *The shoes!* Sapphire would jump at any chance to prance around in those platforms.

"Sapphire, would you do me a *huge* favor?" I implored. "I believe we just got in some anal products—they should be stacked on the bottom of that glass display if there are any left. Would you be so kind as to walk the gentleman over there?"

With Sapphire's attention averted, the situation had been successfully de-escalated, and as expected, parading around even such a short distance was too tempting for Sapphire to resist. "C'mon, honey!" Sapphire bossed the customer. "I've been looking for something new, myself. Let's see what I can find. Besides, this conversation is getting stale anyway!"

Appearing afraid to defy Sapphire's direct order, the customer reluctantly did as he was told. As he turned to glance at me, I nodded to indicate it was safe to go, and off he went, dwarfed by his outspoken tour guide.

Meanwhile back at the desk, Isaac playfully caressed his wavy shoulder-length hair. "I thought she would never leave," he gasped with relief. "I think the hormones are making her delusional."

"I *know* you are not talking about me!" a voice echoed from across the room. Apparently, those hormones were also increasing Sapphire's hearing. "You wait until I come back over there."

Why, Isaac? I thought, looking at him and shaking my head. "You just had to go there, didn't you?"

Isaac clicked his compact closed and placed it in his bag, which he was now searching for other items. "You would never guess we had a *thing*, based on how much we bicker and argue, huh?"

"It was a very *short* thing," Sapphire's voice once again rang out from the distance.

"What are you, bionic?" I shouted. "Jamie Summers had nothing on this one!"

Isaac opened a tube of chap-stick and strategically dotted his lips. "No, she is just nosy and likes to ear hustle ... and she can't resist putting in her two cents—even when she only has a penny."

"Uh-uh, bitch, I know you did not just—"

"You know, I *can* believe you two were involved, actually," I swiftly interrupted. "You definitely fight like a couple ... of *girls!*"

As expected, the customer I had sent on the not-so-wild goose chase didn't find what he had been looking for and returned to the counter to pay for his product. Once the transaction was complete, he dashed for the exit, certainly slightly traumatized by the experience.

Luckily for me (and Isaac), Sapphire was busy taking advantage of the large circular over-head mirror hanging in the corner of the store. Isaac leaned in and whispered to me. "I don't know what I was thinking. ... She isn't even my *type*."

I whispered back, "What *is* your type?"

"I like white boys, some Hispanics—depending on how they look."

"Look?"

"Yes, I want someone who is clean-cut, handsome, and respectful. I don't go for the *pelons* or *cholos* with the shaved heads and tattoos. That's why I don't date black guys. I seem to come across too many wannabe thugs."

"Well, Sapphire is far from *all* those things!" I said.

"Right?! … I think it's because she 'looks' like a woman. I am attracted to women—just not what's between their legs."

"It's funny hearing that from a guy," I admitted. "Ask a lot of women and they will say the opposite: *All* that most men are interested in is what's between their legs."

"Eww, no!" Isaac grimaced, face wrinkled. "It's disgusting."

At the risk of sounding *too* vulgar, I asked, "so you prefer—an asshole?"

"Well, I am the female in the relationship … and I keep *this* fresh and clean. Besides, a pussy gets too gushy and wet. I can lubricate myself just the right amount. Not to mention, a pussy can never be *this* tight."

"Are you speaking from experience or opinion?"

"Personal experience. I had a girlfriend in high school, and that was the last time I had sex with a female."

"That's not a very large sample size."

"Ha-ha. It wasn't just that. That's around the time I learned I preferred boys to girls."

"Really, I've never heard this story," Sapphire chimed in, his brief self-admiration session over. "Now you have to spit it out," I coaxed, egging Isaac on.

"Spitting is rude—I'm a swallower."

There is sharing, there is TMI (too much information) … and then there is *that!* "Honey, tell me something I don't know," Sapphire said. "Get to the story." It was my turn to breathe a sigh of relief, because I had *no* words.

"I was fifteen at the time, had a girlfriend, and was 'straight as an arrow,'" Isaac shared, playing with his hair once again. "Or at least I *thought* I was."

"Honey please, my gaydar would have picked up on that right away!"

"*Anyways*," said Isaac, brushing off the comment, "she started catching me looking at guys. I would tell her I was checking out their outfits. That should have given away my preference right there!"

"*Okay?!*" Sapphire agreed.

"Once I saw Antonio Sabato Jr., that was it." The vision in Isaac's head of the one-time heartthrob produced a wicked smile. "I noticed something was 'rising up' down *there* and thought, *Should this be happening?* At first, I admired his physical conditioning and athleticism—then it grew into attraction. I had this huge poster of him—which my girl hated."

"Honey, she was young and dumb, getting jealous over a piece of paper?"

"The funny part is, she didn't want me lusting over the image of another person, but she introduced the idea of having a foursome."

Upon hearing that tidbit of information, Sapphire retracted his previous statement. "I take that back, she wasn't dumb. She was *very* smart! That girl realized how you were and took advantage of that situation to get her freak on."

Begrudgingly, I admitted, "I've always said women are smarter than men."

"Yes, we are, honey!"

"He's talking about the ones with ovaries!" Isaac intervened at the risk of raising Sapphire's ire.

"That is your *second* strike," Sapphire warned. "You *do not* want three!"

"*Please*! As I was saying, I thought it would be 'traditional' in the sense of a girl for me and guy for her. Turns out, it was a girl—who she was secretly seeing behind my back—for her and that girl's ex-boyfriend for me!"

"Ooh, child, like I said, girl's smart *and a freak*, OKAY?!"

True and very true.

"One day, she told me she had friends coming over," Isaac continued. "They came inside and sat down in the living room, then she took me in the kitchen and just *sprung* the idea on me."

"How did you react?" I asked.

"I am conservative, so I didn't go for it—at first. But we went back in the room and my girlfriend started making out with the girl ... and then the guy joined in."

"*Awkward*, third wheel!" Sapphire chimed in.

"Right?!" Isaac concurred. "But then he motioned for me to come sit next to them—which I did. He started touching me. It was weird but *exciting* at the same time. My gut was wrenching to the point I eventually got up and left the room."

With thoughts of the inner turmoil he had experienced still bringing obvious discomfort, Isaac clutched his stomach and averted his gaze downward. "I smoked a blunt and drank some José Cuervo, which helped me blow off steam. It was the only way I knew how to deal with all the doubts and questions that ran through my mind."

Sapphire was a surprising source of sympathy. "You poor thing. That first moment you realize you're different from what you have known can be life-changing." Life-changing, indeed. People have been known to commit suicide because they didn't know how to effectively cope with feelings such as these or deal with the possible consequences of their future choices.

The more I listened to the exchange between Sapphire and Isaac, I realized any venue can serve as a makeshift classroom. Any individual can assume the role of teacher, if those around are willing to focus on the message and not fixate on the messenger. Society tends to ostracize those who are different, but if we were all alike, what could we teach one other? How could we learn anything new, as I was?

"The guy came into the kitchen—and basically started to seduce me," Isaac recollected, "but not in the 'usual' way. He made me feel more comfortable by asking questions and allowing me to talk and hear my thoughts aloud. I felt stimulated, but shy because I'd never experienced anything like this and didn't know what to do with a guy."

Sapphire simply being Sapphire, said, "Girl, just let nature take over. You are who you are. Like I always say, what doesn't come out in the wash *will* come out in the rinse."

The angst Isaac had initially felt gave way to appreciation as he remembered his admirer's careful treatment of the situation. "'You've seen lesbians' is what he said to me. Next thing you know, my lips are on his lips. ... The girls came in and were like, "Aha, we *knew* it!"

We all got undressed. The girls started going at it, and he was treating me like a princess, being gentle and sweet in the ways a man would love a woman. Then we all joined in."

This would be Isaac's introduction to the swinger lifestyle—yet another aspect of his sexual life that could not have been more different than my own; however, his story's ending would evoke a sentiment we both shared.

"Three months later, I caught him dancing and kissing another man at a club in Los Angeles," Isaac grunted. "That was my first heartbreak. LA is a bitch!"

"Amen!" I agreed. "Been there, felt that!"

"Really?" Sapphire and Isaac queried in unison, brows raised.

"Yes, I ... oh please—not the whole caught-my-boyfriend-kissing-another-man thing. I was referring to the description of LA."

Isaac winked coyly at Sapphire. "You know, Dré ... I normally don't do black guys, but I would make an exception for you, sexy chocolate man!"

"A person really has to watch what they say around you two," I muttered. "One bionic, the other bisexual."

Isaac flashed me a smile while zipping up his handbag. Glancing at his watch, he signaled to Sapphire, and they began gathering their things. Isaac then provided further clarification. "Dré, the difference for me in terms of my attraction to the sexes is this: I can kiss a beautiful woman and not get aroused, but if I kiss a hot guy, I will get excited!"

Sapphire required a summation. "So basically, what did you learn from the whole experience?"

"It showed me what I wanted and helped me define who I really am," Isaac declared, placing a hand over his heart. "I learned I could be friends with women—but my heart belongs to men."

Speaking of men, one came through the door, passing by Isaac and Sapphire. Had he not been so preoccupied with his cell-phone conversation, he would have noticed the look of disapproval from the two resident fashion police.

"Weirdo! Time to go, honey!"

Reaching out to shake my hand, Isaac said, "Good-bye, chocolate man ... and thank you for the talk. I enjoyed it."

"Likewise. See you girls later."

"Yes you will!" they shouted together.

Well, I had made it through another shop experience—barely! Three o' clock couldn't come fast enough. This gentleman should be my final customer. The girls must have been rubbing off on me, because all I could think as he approached was *That's a hideous shirt!*

The customer placed a video on the counter while continuing to talk on the phone, sharing the conversation with all in earshot. Apparently on his way into the store, another man had asked if he wanted some company. And of course, he spared no detail in describing his brief "encounter" with Sapphire and Isaac to whomever he had on the phone.

When he finally finished his conversation, he turned his attention to the matter at hand. "What do I owe you?"

"Twenty-two even."

As he dug through his pocket, I could hear the crinkling of crisp dollar bills. Along with his payment came a brief assessment of the establishment. "Man, there are some weirdos around here!"

Poignantly, I broke the news to him. "Funny you should mention that, sir ... because that's what a customer just said about you!"

"Me?!"

OH MAN(NEQUIN)!

The decade of the 2000s is responsible for the explosion of the Crime Scene Investigation (CSI) series on television. CSI-themed programming is still going strong, the only major change being the city location: New York. Miami. Las Vegas. CSI has even gone cyber!

Apparently, however, San Diego doesn't suffer from criminal activity worthy of television recognition. (Not that I'm complaining.) I admit, when one thinks violent crime, this city probably doesn't come to mind, but that's not to say San Diego doesn't have its fair share of "incidents." If investigators ever came to our shop searching for DNA, we need only point them in the direction of our two most popular employees: the mannequins. On any given day, a Peek-A-Boo tube dress lifted off one of our statuesque workers could provide prints galore. Both male and female alike have shown a healthy appreciation for our girls.

"I love her tits!" an admiring woman once said while fondling the mannequin's bust like an infatuated frat boy. Not wanting to be bested by her inanimate counter-part, she then turned to me for validation (much to my surprise) and lifted her shirt (much to my delight.) "I know you see boobs all the time. ... Do you think mine are as nice as hers?" she asked. Definitely not my worst moment behind the counter. I mean, a guy should get a perk (or two) every now and then, right?!

Besides, this is one of those female-trap questions where the answer is so obvious, a guy could completely get it wrong by overthinking. You know, right up there with "Do I look fat in this dress?" Fortunately for me in this case, I had no reason to lie. "Absolutely!" was my vigorous response to her, which drew an immediate smile.

"How ya likes them apples?!" her boyfriend bragged. "Not bad, huh?"

Melons would have been a more fruit-worthy comparison, but we were nevertheless in agreement. "Uh—not bad at all!" I replied.

On another occasion, a man came stumbling into the store from the bar next door in a drunken stupor. He began undressing the mannequin (which wouldn't take very long) with his eyes. His hands soon followed. "She doesn't need a breast exam, so would you kindly remove your hands and back away from the merchandise?" I instructed. We are very protective of our working girls, so groping is highly frowned upon by the staff.

His speech slurred, he said, "Sorry, bro; she is just so *hot*! I'd love to take her home."

"I don't think you can afford her."

"How much?"

"Two hundred and fifty dollars."

"Bullshit!"

"Real shit! Check the price tag on the stand."

"Aw, man. ... I could go over to El Cajon Boulevard and get a hooker for the whole night for that price."

"Happy hunting! And in your condition—best of luck! I've got some pills—and condoms—I'm sure you would be needing. Other than that, hands off the merchandise!"

You must understand, most of the clerks (including myself) share a special bond with the ladies. I've known them longer than most of my coworkers. They were here years ago when I first started as store manager. Everything I have seen and heard, they have as well—and more! At times, it seems as if the mannequins and I are the only sane ones in the building—which is quite a statement.

Angelina and Devin are responsible for the mannequins' upkeep, making sure outfits are sharp, wigs are neatly brushed, and accessories perfectly accentuate various looks. Whether it be Swedish nurse, French maid, or red-haired dominatrix, our life-size Barbies rely upon these two to stay—as Tara Banks used to say—*fierce!*

Angelina likes to paint their nails and adorn them with costume jewelry. I've seen Devin talking to the mannequins while changing their clothes. He has even gone so far as to give them names: Tiffany and Tori. (I think working graveyard has finally gotten to him.) There is even discussion of creating a web page on a social networking site and posting pictures of them in different outfits. This would be a great way to display our lingerie to a widespread audience while making our girls in-house celebrities.

"I kinda hinted the idea to the owner and he liked it," Angelina said. "It would be fun to see how people responded to our work—and it would make the store money. What do you think?"

I agreed that it could only help business; however, I did provide a cautionary tale—one suitable for the *Twilight Zone* ... or perhaps better for *America's Most Wanted*!

With Angelina's full attention, I repeated a story told to me by Kenneth, a personnel manager who had worked for the company for over fifteen years. When I first heard the story, I couldn't believe it. So to say I was anxious to see Angelica's reaction would certainly be an understatement.

"This guy came into our store one day wanting to purchase a mannequin," Kenneth had said during a phone conversation we'd had a while back. "I told the guy our mannequins weren't for sale, but the owner overheard the conversation and told me, 'Everything is for sale!'" (Basically, our company motto is "If it's in the store and it's inanimate, it can be purchased!")

Kenneth continued, "So the guy winds up talking to the owner for a few minutes and the next thing I know, he's telling me he will be back tomorrow to pick up the mannequin. Sure enough, the next day, he pulled up in a van. He came in the store, bought a wig and some clothes, then purchased the mannequin for $300."

"Nothing sounds out of the ordinary," Angelina interrupted my telling.

I simply smiled, not wanting to give anything away, knowing she wasn't at all prepared for what she was about to hear, for Kenneth had made a startling discovery upon assisting the customer to the van with his new merchandise: "When the guy slid open the door, there were about eight other mannequins inside."

A brief pause provided the dramatic effect. Angelina's face wrinkled in confusion. The setup was perfectly done. "Tell me, tell me," she insisted, laughing at her own impatience. "What happened?"

As the gentleman sifted through the artificial bodies to make room for his newest passenger, Kenneth inquired about why the van was littered with mannequins. "Do you own a department store or something?"

Chuckling, I pretended not to see the depravity of the situation.

"What's the matter, you've never seen a real-life woodpecker before?"

Angelina covered her mouth with both hands to keep from laughing aloud. "Some people shouldn't even be allowed out in public," she giggled.

"You see what could be waiting out there for our girls," I warned. "Do we really want to risk exposing them to the leader of some sordid mannequin sex ring?"

Angelina walked over to Tiffany and promptly ripped the price tag off the base, saying, "That's it!" She then walked in Tori's direction.

"Our girls are not for sale! They are not leaving this store—and that's *final!*"

"That's a bit drastic, Angelina, don't you think? Besides, Devin assured me the day he quits, he is taking the mannequins with him."

"Oh—so they're better off in the hands of the guy who names them and *talks* to them everyday?"

"Touché. Off with the tags!"

OTTERS AND COUGARS AND BEARS— OH MY!

Snake. Rat. Pig. If one of these descriptions is assigned to an individual, a clear and concise image is drawn of that person. And now, there is a new label— one that has gained notoriety over the past fifteen years, thanks to the dating practices of popular stars such as Madonna, Demi Moore, and, more recently, Kris Jenner: cougar.

This is a slang term for a woman who seeks sexual relations with a man who is considerably younger than herself.[9] The age difference can be as small as seven years and as significant as thirty.

In reality, cougars are known to be—in addition to exceptionally graceful and beautiful—-excellent stalk-and-ambush predators. In most cases, the same can be said about these sexual dynamos who enjoy "drinking from the fountain of youth."

Since art imitates life, shows such as *Desperate Housewives* and *Cougar Town* came to reflect this wildly popular dating practice. Following suit as only the porn world can, titles like *The Cougar Chronicles* and *To Catch a Cougar* soon made their way to XXX shelves. Just as it is in the wild, however, the societal cougar is not the only hunter in the dating jungle. She often can—and will—find herself in competition with other sexually charged predators who are equally bold and determined.

"Do you know about bears, cubs, or wolves?" Jim asked me. "We have lots of labels in our lifestyle—and they aren't all animal-related!"

---

[9] "Cougar (slang)". In *Wikipedia, The Free Encyclopedia*. 27 July 2016, https://en.wikipedia.org/w/index.php?title=Cougar_(slang)&oldid=731848552.

Jim is a regular who also is gay. He had shared a few stories before, so I knew whatever he was about to say could possibly have me looking at these creatures in a different light.

"All I know is what I see on the gay box covers," I answered. "And I don't closely examine them—if you catch my drift."

"Then this will be educational—and fun," he replied.

"I don't know about the latter."

Being from Chicago, I was used to the Bears being a football team and the Cubs one of the city's two baseball franchises—the White Sox being the other—but I knew sports had nothing to do with Jim's tutorial.

"A bear is a big, burly, hairy gay man, and a cub is a bear in the making," Jim explained. "Bears and cubs can couple. In fact, they usually do."

"By 'couple,' you mean …"

"Yes."

Dorothy was starting to realize she wasn't in Kansas anymore. "So about a week ago, I saw a guy pull up in a Range Rover," I told Jim. "His license plate read, 'GLAM CUB.' Now the moniker—coupled with his appearance—makes sense!"

"So, on a gay scale of one to ten," Jim guessed, "he was about a, what, fifteen?"

"Upwards of twenty."

Jim then got even wilder in his animal descriptions. "A wolf is a semi-hairy gay man who is lean and muscular. They are very attractive and sexually aggressive." I could tell from the twinkle in Jim's eye and the excitement in his voice that he'd had favorable encounters with a wolf or two in his day. "A good example of the look of a silver or gray wolf would be Hugh Jackman," he said.

"Thanks, Jim. I will never be able to look at Wolverine the same."

"Lord knows I didn't after seeing him shirtless!"

"Is nothing sacred to you?"

"André, look where you work."

"Touché. ... continue."

Jim did. "An otter is a hairy, non-burly, considerably smaller version of a bear. Very roundish, flat features—and short."

"So homosexual men want otters and heterosexual men chase *beavers*!"

"And how do you like your *beaver*, André?"

"Shaven."

"You heteros have strange preferences."

I was not even going there.

Jim was a portly fellow, Caucasian, mid-forties, not quite six feet tall, and balding, with a scruffy beard that seemed to gray a little more each time I saw him. "So based on the information you have provided, I presume that makes you a bear, Jim?"

"Correct, young man. But I don't do cubs—I prefer twinks."

"You're not referring to a Hostess snack, by chance?"

"No."

"Just checking."

"Twinks are young gay boys, anywhere from eighteen to twenty-four years old. Usually very skinny. Look very young. Some apply makeup and foundation—and think the world revolves around them!"

"Experienced a few of those on the straight side of the dating spectrum," I admitted. "High maintenance knows neither gender nor sexual preference."

"Even though I like the young ones," Jim acknowledged, "sometimes a twunk is easier to deal with."

"A what?"

"A twunk!"

"Are you trying to say trunk?"

"No, I mean *twunk!*"

"A *twunk?*"

"Yes, a ... very funny, André. Do I really sound like Elmer Fudd?"

"Not at all, you was cally wabbit!"

"A twunk is basically an older, more mature, twink. They are more developed physically and mentally and are usually past all the drama."

"Earlier you mentioned something about nonanimal-related labels," I reminded Jim hesitantly. "I suppose our discussion of the twink was the equivalent of adding sugar to cough syrup: get the sweet taste before the bitter." No sooner had I heard myself speak the words than Jim spoke.

"You have such an interesting way of phrasing things, André—however, it's all sweet to me."

I wished I could take the words back!

"Of course you are familiar with the words rice, potato, and burrito?" We had officially moved on to food.

"Yes, Jim."

"Good. Rice is a description for an Asian man; potato is what we call white men; and a burrito is a Mexican male."

"So much for political correctness!"

"Hey, I don't make the terms up; I just know what they mean."

"Don't shoot the messenger, right?"

"Only if it's in the face with a load of—"

"Got it!"

The ensuing exchange belonged on the inside of a Bazooka bubblegum wrapper.

"What do you call a white guy with a white guy?" Jim asked.

"I don't know."

"Mashed potatoes."

"That's kinda funny," I admitted.

"What do you call an Asian with an Asian?"

"I don't know."

"Sticky rice."

"That's kinda gross," I said. I laughed for few minutes (but I didn't eat Chinese for a few weeks).

Jim was not at all impressed with my efforts. "You're not doing very well at this game, André."

"Glad to disappoint you. I haven't exactly been *trying!*"

"Okay, I will give you an easy one—it even has multiple answers."

"Fantastic."

"What do you call a woman who is best friends with a gay man?"

I knew this one! I had been an avid *Will & Grace*-watcher back in the day. I just needed to channel my inner Jack to find the answer. ... *Got it!* "A fag hag!" I shouted.

Unfortunately, my enthusiastic response drew a few unwanted stares. "Sorry, folks! Keep shopping."

Jim clapped sarcastically. "Yes, that's right! They are also called a fairy Mary or a fruit fly."

I was on a roll, so I decided to press my luck. "All right, ask me another!"

"Oh, look at Mr. Confident after getting one right."

"Damn straight!"

"Damn *not!*"

"Okay, I see where you went with that. Good one."

"I'm better than *good*, sir."

"Unbelievable! Why is it that most of the gay men I know can take a completely innocent comment and turn it into something sexual?"

"Isn't that what you heteros do to women?"

"Touché again." *Damn, he is better than good.* Time to redirect the bull. "We're not com-paring homos and heteros here, Jimbo. Let's just stick to the script. You were saying …"

"Well, since you're dodging my question, let's talk about the one thing you heteros are obsessed with."

"Care to be more specific? Sexually speaking, that could be anything from threesomes to penis size to porn."

"I'm talking about the only gay group that is socially acceptable to you testosterone-driven heteros," Jim hinted. "Because men always want what they can't have."

Say no more! The "L-word." "Lesbians," I answered.

"Yes sir! If you asked me, lipsticks rule the world! Are you familiar with that term?"

"By lipstick, you mean the ultra-girly, very sexy, smoking-hot ones, right?"

"Those would be the ones."

"I'm a bit foggy. I think I may need further clarification."

First Jim snickered. Then he shook his head. Finally, he indulged me. "It sounds like you have a pretty firm grasp of the concept. I'll just add that—as you clearly exemplify—the guys want them, the girls like them, and the twinks want to be them—minus the vagina, of course."

I told Jim it was a remarkable accomplishment on my part to be having this type of conversation with him; years before, I couldn't have done it. When I started working at the shop, my opinions and views were tainted by the judgments and stereotypes of others; but as time went by, I interacted with individuals of varying sexual orientations and preferences and came to the realization that we're really all the same. I mean, if what someone else believes in and practices doesn't harm myself or anyone else, why should I have a problem with it, right?

Jim smiled at me as a proud father would at his son who had just learned a valuable lesson. "Bravo, sir!" he lauded.

We were briefly interrupted by a gentleman frantically making his way up to the counter. "Excuse me, but do you sell any amateur porn?"

"There is really no such thing as amateur porn these days, sir," I said. "Camera phones have made certain of that. All the girls you see on these box covers have been recorded having sex in some form or fashion."

"Well, have you heard of a company called Homegrown? Apparently, they specialize in amateur porn."

"Yes, we have a few of their titles. Are you looking for one in particular?"

"Yes—the one with my wife in it!"

"Excuse me?"

"About three years ago, I found out my wife was making porno movies at our house while I was out working. And she was fucking my best friend!"

Upon hearing that tidbit of information, Jim put his hand to his chest as if he'd swallowed something that wouldn't go down. (It was safe to think that but not say out loud.)

"Uh—okay," I mumbled. "Well, we definitely don't have anything that old. Maybe I could find her by the name she used."

Scratching his head, he said, "She went by different ones: Ice ... umm Exstacy, Ms. Money-maker." While rattling off her aliases, the regret in his voice became more and more evident.

A look of anguish unsuccessfully tried to mask his shame. "I knew I married her too soon. She ruined my career as a law officer. I confronted my best friend a few times before he finally admitted to what was going on—and he did so only after I played a video clip on my phone that a few of my partners showed me—so I would believe it."

(That must have been beyond humiliating.)

Unfortunately for him, most of his wife's appearances had been only posted on the Internet and this "best friend" happened to work in the adult industry and had been successful in getting the footage removed. The customer wanted a copy of her "work" for a very specific reason: "I'm trying to win custody of our son. That bitch took enough from me. I'm not letting her have my son!"

I noticed Jim was getting a bit choked up, his emotions getting the best of him. It was obvious he was a bear all right—a big ole teddy bear!

Obviously, it would be up to me to figure out how to "skin this cat"! I offered a suggestion: "Probably your best bet is to go the Homegrown website and see if you can order a copy of the video. Your 'friend' may have removed the movies from the Internet, but I seriously doubt he bought all the copies of the videos from the company. If you aren't having any luck, come back here and I'll talk to our buyer to see if he can find something."

"That's a good idea! Thanks, bro, I appreciate it. I still can't believe she did that shit to me. I thought she was a great woman, but she turned out to be a real snake!"

Jim and I looked at each other. *Yahtzee!*

SLIP-SLIDIN' AWAY

We all know that eventually, we cross paths with people who will leave indelible marks in our lives; we just have to hope that the impressions left are favorable. In my case, Sapphire was one such person—and our encounters were certainly memorable for all the right reasons. Whether I was seeing an interaction between him and someone else or having a one-on-one conversation with him, the experience was always entertaining.

In one such instance, we stood across the counter from each other, playing the waiting game: me for three 'o clock and him for a ride home. As I was learning, idle time with a trans-sexual can prove to be a dangerous thing. "You know ... I'm thinking about writing my own book," Sapphire disclosed. "And I am going to come talk to you for help."

I was flattered yet somewhat fearful. "I'm afraid I'm not done recovering from some of the things you've already told me—and that's just surface stuff! I don't know if I could handle you getting *deep* on me."

"Well let's find out! I have about forty-five minutes before I have to go." At this amusement park of a job, Sapphire's stories would be considered an "E-ticket" ride; and just like the moment you get on that nausea-inducing roller coaster and the safety bar locks you in, my apprehension was building. I knew the experience would be well worth it, however.

And so the ride began.

"Unlike some people who suffer from confusion about their sexuality, I've always known about myself," Sapphire started. "I used to have dreams about grown men as a kid."

This deer's eyes widened as it stared straight ahead into the bright lights of impending danger, but no brakes were applied.

"I'm not playing," he continued. "I am serious! My dad used to have a sex book and I would always find the man more interesting because with women—nothing was there."

I was roadkill.

"It's funny how life will let you know who you are … you just have to listen. You may not get your answer right away, but eventually, you'll have it."

"As you know," I interjected, "God works in mysterious ways."

Although Sapphire had quickly come to terms with his sexuality, it had taken a while before his parents had. "I think my mom always knew," Sapphire determined. "Her perception was that someone had messed with me, which wasn't the case. They wanted me to stop switching when I walked—but I couldn't."

"What about your dad?"

"I couldn't talk to my father about it until I was thirty years old. When we finally talked, he told me I didn't choose him and he didn't choose me and these are the cards we were dealt—and so we make them work! Today he is so accepting. Both sides of my family are, really."

I questioned him skeptically. "You mean none of your family members expressed any type of negativity?"

"Actually ... my uncle is still getting used to it. He is a pastor. He's coming around, but I ease into things slowly with him. You can't press the older generation."

What I didn't doubt was the fact that Sapphire had come across a few individuals from the past who had helped shape the person he was presently—one in particular.

"Michael," he whispered fondly.

"Who's Michael?"

"*Michael* is ... I didn't have anyone to look up to growing up. I came out my senior year in high school, and that experience was eye-opening for me. Sometimes I feel like I'm still searching. Learning me."

"I think we all are," I attested.

"True. But Michael helped me realize my self-worth. He brought me orchids. Wrote me poems. Eventually, he even took me snorkeling and surfing. We did things I wouldn't normally do. I felt that was really cool."

"So what happened?"

"I found out he was a *trick*!"

"Huh?"

"Yes! He had dated the other trannies, but not to the extent he did with me. He was even going to get me an apartment! But he ended up going back to his wife."

"He was married?!"

"Yes. She had cancer, and if I was the wife, I wouldn't want someone doing that to me. Eventually, he ended up passing away too. The experience really taught me to be considerate of other people's situations."

Despite the way things had ended, Sapphire still reminisced on his time with Michael with great appreciation.

"I'm so glad he came into my life. I remember the day I noticed him staring at me from afar. He walked up to me and asked if I was dating. At first, I didn't know this was the terminology for working. When I figured it out, I told him yes and he asked how much. When I told him, he shook his head and said I was undervaluing myself. He offered me $350 just to keep him company."

Smugly, I asked, "Uh-huh ... doing what?"

"Well, *hello*, Mr. Implication!"

"We both know nobody gets something for nothing! Especially $350 worth of something."

"Look, honey, all Michael wanted was for me to keep him company."

"That's *all*, huh? In a second, I am going to become Mr. Accusation."

"Well ... we would mess around a little."

"*Now* we're getting somewhere."

"But it wasn't like that *all* the time. Here, I will break it down for you."

"No, that really isn't necessary."

"Listen, honey, *you* ordered the drink, so take the shot!"

I could use a swig of something strong right about then— Hennessey on the rocks, perhaps!

"So, Michael would invite me to his hotel room to watch him put on women's clothes, but he was a cross-dresser who liked to *fuck*, not *get fucked!*"

Make it Jack Daniels, straight up!

"But as I said before, Michael took me out of my comfort zone, which allowed me to learn so much more about myself. Now I understand that as long as I know who I am, where I'm from, and where I'm going, nothing else matters."

"You attribute all that to meeting him? Wow, we should all have a Michael in our lives." *Did I just say that? Dammit. Open mouth, insert foot. Backpedal quickly.*

"What I mean is—"

"I *know* what you mean, honey." Sapphire's reassurance was accompanied by a subtle wink—a gesture that didn't go unnoticed.

"Was that really necessary?"

"Yes. Your borderline homophobia is so cute!"

"Glad you think so."

"But seriously," Sapphire resumed saying, "dirty clothes, holey clothes, it doesn't matter. I still walk like royalty. People compliment me on the way I carry myself, and I *love* the attention. I get in heels and sexy clothes and give you body, attitude, *all that*! But no matter what I put on, this face stays the same."

"I'm sure you didn't develop that *swag* overnight?"

"No, my skin has gotten a lot thicker over the course of time—you can imagine the dirty names people have called me—so instead of getting angry, I use sarcasm as my defense mechanism."

"It's quite a wonderful tool, is it not?!"

"Oh yes! It allows me to deflect quickly and very matter-of-factly. You will never see me break down—in public, anyway."

If someone wasn't calling Sapphire by his name, I was curious as to what gender pronoun he preferred when being addressed. As it turns out, he came up with his own simple yet clever term.

"My nieces and nephews call me shim, which is a she-him," he explained. "It's a sign of respect. Hermaphrodites live with both parts, *right*? You can't call them a man one day and a woman the next. My relatives can't call me uncle one day and auntie the next. They can't refer to me as one or the other depending upon how I'm dressed. That would be too confusing! So, I came up with shim. I wish instead of being stuck on labels, society would realize people are human and should be treated accordingly. There is no prize for guessing a person's sexuality."

In a perfect world, things would operate in such a manner—on a plane of existence we have not yet reached, a higher level of consciousness we have not yet attained—but the benefit to living in a society plagued by ass-backwards thinking is a surplus of writing material.

"Did I ever tell you about the time I got locked up?" Sapphire asked. "I was terrified when I was incarcerated, but after being there, it was as enjoyable as the time I've spent free. The hellish part was how I got arrested!"

My curiosity now gave way to suspense, like that you feel on a roller coaster as it begins its slow steady climb before finally perching on the top rail.

"While waiting for the trolley, I went inside a convenience store to buy a Dove bar. My trolley was coming, so I placed a $10 bill on the counter and headed out."

"You didn't want your change?" I inquired. "You were willing to pay ten dollars for something that costs $1.50?"

"Honey, I was dead tired and in a hurry. All I wanted to do was get home."

Supposedly, the security guard didn't see Sapphire pay for the item and ran outside to confront him. Blocking Sapphire's path, he then went to put Sapphire's hands behind his back.

"I was not going for that, so we struggled a bit—then the trolley officers showed up," Sapphire remembered. "At this point, they are all trying to restrain me and not listen to my explanation. Adrenaline kicked in, and I started fighting back. Next thing I know, eight cops are hog-tying me and blasting me with pepper spray!"

The roller coaster makes a gravity-defying drop.

"It felt like someone poured gasoline on my skin. My mouth was dry and burning ... all I wanted to do was spit! One of the officers said if I kept it up, he was going to hit me in the throat!"

Because of his actions, Sapphire found himself in police custody, sitting in a chair, restrained by a net. "It all happened so fast ... I'm thinking the entire time, *How in the world did everything come down to this?!*"

The judge who heard the case did not appreciate Sapphire's antics nor his repeated court-room appearances—a fact he let be known. "The judge said he was tired of seeing me and thought I needed to learn a lesson," Sapphire stated. "He gave me one year with the possibility of serving only six months with good behavior. I had some priors that factored into my sentencing, as well as the fact that I had resisted arrest. I could have fought it, but it was my word against eight officers! And if I lost, I would serve more time, so off I went."

Spiral loop.

"The first thing I remember was an officer giving me a bulky pair of nail clippers and telling me to cut my nails," Sapphire said. "Honey, I cried! He told me if he ever saw my nails that length again, I would get a charge!"

"Why?"

"Because they could be considered as deadly weapons."

Serving a prison sentence is very different from doing jail time, according to Sapphire. He told me that in jail, trannies are kept separate from general population to "help avoid incidents and complications," but prison is not this way. Groups form voluntarily along racial, regional, and sexual lines. "Trannies stick together for survival, just like the other groups," he revealed. This was how he came across a few friendly faces—and another influential presence in his life.

"I ran into some of the people I knew on the outside, including Tina," he said. "She was very good to me. She helped me get a lot of the comforts I enjoyed, like nail polish, lotion, Vaseline, and a perm kit. We were all like a little family! I know it sounds crazy, but it's amazing how bonds develop during different situations. And … this is where I met my first boyfriend."

Second spiral loop.

"I never had someone take care of me the way Rob did," Sapphire proclaimed. "I wanted for nothing. He protected me in ways I didn't even realize. Nobody dared mess with me, because they knew I was with him."

Epiphanies can occur in the weirdest of places and at the oddest of times, and it seems those who are incarcerated tend to experience these profound revelations the most—including Sapphire. "It's funny, but I found someone on the inside that treated me the way I wanted someone to treat me on the outside. That was my first *real* relationship!"

Unfortunately, another commonality between prison and the free world is infidelity. No matter who, where, when, or why, we all seem to share the urge to "explore."

"Even though my bond with (Rob) kept getting stronger, I would still flirt with other guys,"

Sapphire admitted. "I was young and surrounded by good-looking, muscular men. I felt like a kid in a candy store. I only cheated on him once—with the guy who was doing my tattoo."

Sapphire also learned that although women are usually associated with it, men also like to gossip. "The tattooist must have talked to his boys about what happened, because we were the only two in the cell and we had to be discreet because guards were walking by the entire time."

Regardless, it would be only a matter of time before Rob found out because, according to Sapphire, nobody kept secrets from him. "He always kept eyes on me. I would have conversations with people when he wasn't around, and when I'd see him, he'd ask me what I was talking about with that person. Prison is like the outside world, but it's more closely knit. Everyone knows everyone, so you can't hide things— especially with someone who was respected the way he was."

After a few hairpin turns, the roller coaster hit the designated straightaway, finally giving its lone passenger time to catch his breath; but like on any good ride, the straightaway wasn't the end, just a precursor to the big finish. Another man's tale would provide the final thrill of this trip, however.

No sooner than Sapphire had finished telling his story, Phil came walking through the door. It was almost three o'clock, quitting time. After Phil and Sapphire had exchanged pleasantries, we proceeded with the shift change. As Phil thumbed through dollar bills and assorted change, he asked, "Did you hear what happened the other night?"

Just when I thought the ride was over, the roller coaster creaked its way upward, once again, stopping at its apex.

"Regarding what, Phil?" I asked.

"This customer brought some mag-packs up to the counter, waited until I had come off the floor and closed the door behind me— then dashed out the store!"

Free fall!

"Ooh, honey!" Sapphire shouted.

"Seriously, Phil? What did you do?"

"I dove across the counter and managed to grab hold of him as he was heading out the door!"

The roller coaster does a triple loop! "Good, you caught him!" I presumed.

"No! Unfortunately, not! He was so lubed up that he slid right through my hands and I fell to the floor!"

Phil has several Captain America tee shirts that he often wears to work. The outfit must have gone to his head, as he attempted to imitate the "Star-Spangled Avenger!" He explained, "I got up and ran out the door after the guy. I tried to tackle him in the middle of the street. I grabbed him by his free arm, but his jacket slid right off his body and I fell to the ground holding nothing but a windbreaker!"

Curses! Foiled again.

"I realized I had left the store unattended, so I picked up a few of the mags he had dropped and headed back."

Ride over.

"Oh, there is my cousin outside!" Sapphire shouted. "I will see you guys later. I'm sorry, Phil." Sapphire pointed to me. "And you, mister ... I will be back to discuss *my* book!"

Phil stopped counting the register long enough to look up at me. "A *book*? She's writing a book? That's a trip!"

I continued filling out my paperwork and grinned. "Helluva ride!"

JURASSIC PORN

June 1993. In Hollywood, this time of year meant one thing: blockbuster season! Billboards of big-money feature films were splashed across the LA skyline. A cartoon drawing of what looked like a prehistoric animal was plastered on the side of a building. No title was above the picture, simply a release date below it. The advertisement was for the highly anticipated Steven Spielberg release Jurassic Park. Soon, the dinosaurs represented by that symbol would recapture the American imagination.

Prehistoric predators like the Allosaurus and Tyrannosaurus would become household names, but none more than the Velociraptor. It quickly set itself apart by displaying human-like traits such as cunning, guile, and ruthlessness. (Based upon fossil evidence, many experts believe the Velociraptor in the movie was modeled after the *Deinonychus*.)[10] In the film, security for the compound is compromised when power is temporarily shut off, causing the electric barricades that keep the animals at bay to deactivate. This occurrence allows the dinosaurs—the raptors, in particular—to roam free and wreak havoc.

Fast-forward twenty years to another power outage that happened without warning ... at a moment's notice ... in the blink of an eye ... all the clichés. It was a Saturday night and I was at the store at fifteen minutes 'til midnight. I was pulling an overtime shift. (Events to come would prove I was in the wrong place at the wrong time.) One minute I was in mid-conversation with my coworker Greg about how much the music

---

[10] "10 Facts about Velociraptors," Bob Strauss, About Education, http://dinosaurs.about.com/od/typesofdinosaurs/ss/10-Facts-About-Velociraptor.htm#step2.

sucked these days—you know, the same thing our parents used to say to us when we were younger—and the next minute: *darkness*. No power. Grid down. *Blackout!*

Movies abruptly stopped. Money had been wasted. Big problem! The creatures of the night howled in objection at their nocturnal activities being rudely interrupted. They halt in mid-stroke, caught with their pants down. (Yes, I went there!) Foul sounds emanated from the booths in back. Groaning. Yelling. Swearing. Once again, the raptors were loose!

As I sat there with Greg in a pitch-black room, another year popped into my head: 1775. I thought of the Battle of Bunker Hill because, like those colonists waiting to engage the British Redcoats, we could see the whites of their eyes [11] as they scurried to the front of the store. Eerily, these eyes swam about in a sea of darkness as if independent of bodies. The creatures scampered around in a disgruntled frenzy. "Unfinished business" had left them restless, angry. Horny! We could hear shuffling—the sound of loose items being snatched from the shelves. The dark provided ideal cover for sticky fingers.

Oh no! Not on my watch! Order must be restored, so I reached underneath the counter for assistance in counteracting this wave of aggression. I instructed Greg to go to the back, evacuate the area, and

---

[11] "Battle of Bunker Hill," History.com Staff, 2009, http://www.history.com/topics/american-revolution/battle-of-bunker-hill.

make sure no one was tampering with the bill collectors in the booths, but before I sent him off, I activated my weapon and pierced the blackness with a shining ray from my flashlight. I circulated the beam across the room, randomly freezing bodies in statuesque poses, a la Medusa.

Some threw their hands up to shield their eyes. Others, who were unfortunate enough to be caught gazing directly into the light, shrieked in discomfort. Temporary blindness caused the stirring to momentarily stop. Greg seized the opportunity to slip away safely to the back.

Hold on! There was movement at the counter. I hadn't been quick enough; one had gotten through. I hesitantly told this one that, because of the circumstances, I wouldn't be able to transact any business. I may as well have dangled a fresh piece of raw meat in front of this ravenous carnivore and then quickly snatched it away. She slammed the package on the counter. "You guys need to pay your fuckin' light bill!" she barked as she stomped out of the building. (Coming between a woman and her orgasm is never a good thing!)

The front and rear emergency exit lights finally popped on, providing some illumination. Dissatisfied faces started to come into focus. Their eyes began to adjust. They identified and targeted their prey behind the counter.

The attack began: "I lost ten dollars!" "I had fifteen minutes left on my movie!" "I want my money back!" "I've been traumatized by that flashlight!" "I can't go home without a dildo!"

The ragtag group continued to rush the counter with complaints. The lights had rendered my weapon useless. I still had mace beneath the register, but I would hate to spray a guy who I'd probably helped in the past pick out lingerie for his wife.

I noticed that Greg had successfully herded the wayward flock from the back. He gave me the signal that there were no sheep left behind, and I addressed the angry mob. "Everybody calm down! I reassure those who have spent money that you will be reimbursed for the inconvenience."

"How long will it be?!" one snarled.

"Generally, it only takes a few hours once SDG&E diagnoses the problem. Just come back tomorrow and we will take care of it." With reluctant acceptance, they left, grumbling all the way. Greg escorted them out and collected their information.

It was a little past one o'clock in the morning now, but I made sure to notify all the proper people who need to be contacted in emergencies such as this one. It was late—or early— but they knew that unexpected phone calls are par for the course with a twenty-four- hour operation.

In the middle of explaining to Kenneth what had happened, I heard fidgeting at the side door. That was an emergency exit, so I knew it wasn't Greg, who would enter the store through the main entrance. How had it gotten open? Amid the commotion, had a would-be thief slipped out and left the door ajar?

I told Kenneth I would call him back. I heard Greg call out, "Hey, where are you going?"

A creature deftly made its way back inside the park. It quickly surveyed the area, then proceeded to go about its task, eyes widening with excitement. More of those eyes—I figured I would probably see them in my sleep that night!

The creature's peripheral vision was blocked by a partition, however, so it failed to notice me watching and waiting. It circled around the magazine rack, stopping at the lubes. I circled around my chair, edging toward the door. A large container of lube disappeared from the shelf. A small bottle of mace disappeared from beneath the counter.

Its mission accomplished, the creature turned to make a hasty exit, only to be greeted by the unaccounted-for park keeper. I stared at the claw clutching the unpaid-for item. The creature stared at the hand clutching its consequence. Then our eyes met.

The emergency-exit light blinked intermittently, providing a dramatic countdown to the inevitable in a classic Clint Eastwood moment. My makeshift .357 Magnum in hand, I anxiously awaited its next move. Go ahead, prehistoric punk, make my day!

I looked around. No witnesses. No functioning cameras. I could put this creature on its back with one well-aimed spray and no one would be the wiser. Teach it a lesson! But the keeper's job is to ensure the well-being of the park—and its animals. Such a base act of irresponsibility would go against my own personal code of ethics. But damn, it would feel *really good*!

Greg burst through the front door, abruptly interrupting my thoughts. He surveyed the situation and noticed the apprehensive look in the creature's eyes. He saw my finger tapping on the red safety cap.

"You good?" he asked.

"Never better," I responded, keeping my eyes fixed on the target. I direct the same question to the intruder. "How about you—you good? *Feel lucky?*"

Slowly, it began to walk backward, retracing its steps. It gently placed the bottle back on the glass rack and offered a nervous smile, a sign of submission. It might as well have rolled on its back, claws up! This is generally the part of the exchange when thieves caught red-handed offer up some sort of ridiculous explanation or lame apology, but this one could tell I was not in the mood for either. Outnumbered and weaponless, it remained quiet. A smart decision!

The phone rang.

The creature continued to debate its fate.

The phone rang again.

The park-keeper continued to weigh his options.

The phone rang a third time. Greg continued to wonder if he should answer it.

It was probably Kenneth calling back to check on the status of the store, I figured. Finally, I broke the tension. "Greg, get the phone— and *you*," I said, pointing at the creature, "if I ever catch you in here again, I will spray first and ask how badly your eyes are burning later!" It nodded and looked upon me with relief and gratitude! No sooner than I pushed open the door, it anxiously scampered out into the night.

Unfortunately, the power wouldn't be restored for a few hours. Fortunately for me, however, my shift was ending. We could still hear commotion outside the doors, shouts of frustration echoing against the glass. The cries of angry villagers and torchbearers calling for Frankenstein. Ironically, to this disgruntled mob, I was the monster! But the last of the creatures had already exited the building. The park was secure once again.

50 SHADES OF DRÉ

The 50 Shades of Grey book had a large sect of womankind redefining its ideas about sexuality in regards to the dominant/submissive relationship, though those of us who are in the adult business and/or have participated in the lifestyle know that this dynamic has been a part of the sexual subculture for centuries.

Just before Valentine's Day 2015, the movie 50 *Shades of Grey*, Hollywood's watered-down version of BDSM (bondage & discipline/domination & submission/sadomasochism), hit theaters. Like many other guys, I was dragged to one of the showings by a significant other. She said the book was better than the movie— which usually seems to be the case.

For me, the movie's only point of redemption was a line delivered by one of the main characters, Christian Grey. It was a verbal admission of his state of being, and it stuck with me long after seeing the flick. He stated: "I am fifty shades of fucked up!" This proclamation explained his behaviors as well as the book's title, but it also made me wonder, *How fucked up am I, considering where I have been working the past eight years?* What were the 50 shades of Dré?

As the saying goes, "You are the company you keep." If so, after what I have seen and heard, my shades would number *way* more than fifty, although, unlike Grey, my personal encounters haven't all left me for the worse. I mean, how many people have gotten personal cooking tips from a gourmet chef? Not to mention top-quality meats, fish, and vegetables complete with sure-fire recipes—all for *free!*

Meeting some individuals has even been beneficial to family members. Take Davis, for example. He suffered from marital issues and poor judgment—particularly an indiscretion by the name of Mindy. Through our talks, he eventually focused all his attention on his wife and eliminated other distractions and nonproductive extracurricular activities. As a show of appreciation, Davis made it possible for my mother to see one of her favorite gospel artists, Donnie McClurkin, perform at his local church.

Jacques, who had been the morning janitor and eventually became a good friend and business partner, has a master's degree in business as well as a license to sell real estate. Jacques has also produced and sold music, and he served in the Persian Gulf War. What caused an instant bond between us was the fact that he had at one time managed his own adult store. The stories he told me served to make me feel less paranoid about my own situation.

One such tale involved a time when his boss instructed him to make a delivery to a house in Chula Vista. "I was just out of the Navy and had only been working the job for a few months," Jacques remembered. "I thought this was a common part of the job"—until the deliveries increased in size and frequency. "My boss told me in the beginning not to open the bags—that lasted about two trips!"

Sometimes, it's better not to know.

"The third time I made a delivery, I sat in the car outside the house and curiosity got the best of me. I opened the bag and couldn't believe my eyes!" Highly animated while telling the story, Jacque screamed, "I'm thinking, *Whoa*! What is all this shit?! I'm just a good ole country boy from Georgia. I wasn't used to seeing ball gags, double-ended dildos, and collared leashes!"

It got better. When Jacques went up to the house, he was greeted by a lady dressed in all-white lingerie who noticed the package had been opened. In attempts to satisfy his obvious curiosity, she invited him inside. He cautiously stuck his head in—and that was all the look he needed.

"There were men playing pool naked, women walking around in next to nothing, and couples swapping partners," Jacques observed. "It was my introduction to a swinger's club."

One of the members told Jacques he was welcome back anytime, so when he told his Naval buddies what he had seen and they didn't believe him, he decided to take the stranger up on his offer, yet even with the open invitation, Jacques and his group were still hesitant about going inside. "For two Saturdays in a row, we sat in the car smoking and drinking, trying to build up the courage to do it," Jacques admitted. "When we finally did, it was like four kids in a candy store. None of us *did* anything, but the experience was so new and overwhelming that it's something all of us vividly remember to this day."

Stories like that made my atypical job seem a bit more normal; at the very least, I had met someone who could somewhat relate to my daily dilemmas.

These are some of the people who represent the lighter shades on my adult-experiences palate. They aid in keeping me grounded, help me achieve the balance necessary to keep from being Christian Grey fucked up! The irony, however, is those "darker" shades generally seem to signify the most entertaining experiences, as well as often being the most interesting, the most educational, and the most memorable.

So, in keeping with the *50 Shades* theme, enter the dominatrix.

"I checked out your wall. ... Your selection sucks," a customer complained.

She was a curvy blonde—"thick in all the right places," as they say. She had been observing our fetish wall with great scrutiny and apparent displeasure.

"But I'll take these," she added.

Uh-huh. She was dissatisfied with our lack of variety but "settled" for a ball-gag training system, heavy-duty hog-tie kit, and shock-therapy cock strap. I suppose her first choices would have included a few medieval torture devices.

As she reached inside her wallet, she felt compelled to share some personal information—my not-so-subtle reaction to her items no doubt playing a part. "This isn't the life my parents envisioned for me," she claimed.

"What life would that be?"

"Right," she flippantly remarked. "Well, since you are so *clueless*, I will just say that I am a dominatrix."

"Get outta here!"

She smiled, realizing I was being a smartass—a fact she appreciated—so she played along. "I know, I know. Raised Catholic. Private boarding school. College-educated. Nine-to-five job. But it just wasn't the life for me."

"So you *like* your job?"

"I love it! I couldn't imagine doing anything else!"

Upon hearing this, I asked the obvious follow-up question: "So what made you choose that profession?"

To which she gave the obvious answer: "I hate men!"

"Based on your purchases, I'm inclined to believe that ... as well as think your clients must not be very fond of themselves either."

"Oh they love it! The more painful and humiliating, the better."

This wasn't *exactly* new to me. I had seen men come into the store who liked to be humiliated, but none to the point where physical pain was so welcomed—or even *desired*. Seeing a grown man walk on all fours like a dog or dress up like a schoolgirl (an ugly one, at that) is one thing, but imagining a grown man enjoying having his testicles squeezed in a vise-like grip while being slapped on the ass with a leather strap is a bit harder to digest! I had plenty of judgment there, but as a man, it's difficult to comprehend that experience being pleasurable in any way, shape, or form. But to each his own, I always say—words to fuckin' live by in this business.

As the dominatrix awaited her change, her eyes scanned the contents under the glass countertop. They fixated on one thing after another like a cat watching fish inside a tank. Rhythmically tapping her fingers, she gently sucked on her bottom lip. I dropped the loose coins and receipt in her hand, and she started to walk away. Then suddenly, she stopped.

The cat had spotted something! Her lips curled. Her brow furled. Her ire was raised. The cat screeched, "You guys carry THAT?!" A stiff finger pointed at a copy of *50 Shades of Grey*.

Now, I've owned a few felines in my day and thus understand the best way to settle down an agitated kitty is to stroke it gently, so cautiously, I replied, "You know, as popular as the book is, it does have its detractors,"

I said. "I, for one, was doing some of that stuff way before the book." Yep, Mallory was a freak!

"Without the million-dollar home and jet, of course."

"You and me both, honey!" she replied. "It's a culture here in San Diego. That book is way late!"

"Have you been to the Dungeon, downtown?" I asked.

"I have a dungeon in my home."

"Uh, of course you do—but I am talking about this place where members of the BDSM community get together and play."

"No, never heard of it."

"How about the Crypt over in Hillcrest?"

"Yes, I've been there. They've been bought out, though, by another company."

"Oh, I didn't know that."

Redirecting the topic, she said, "Tell me more about this Dungeon!" she firmly insisted.

Wow! She had quite a presence when barking out a command. It sent a bit of a shiver through me. I could see how men ... err, scratch that. No, I couldn't!

"Well," I resumed, "it's held at a secret location. You must be invited by a regular to gain entrance, think *Eyes Wide Shut*."

Nodding her head, she said, "Understandable. That's a common practice with gatherings of a sensual or sexual nature."

As I told her my story, the memory took me back down that isolated street. It was eight o' clock at night and my companion and I stood outside a garden-variety unlit office building with glass doors at the entrance. It was *unlocked*. Random stragglers made their way off the streets, up the steps, and into the hallway. We all took an elevator up three floors. Upon exiting the elevator, we walked down a long hallway, passing locked door after locked door. I felt like I was going to see the doctor without a scheduled appointment.

We finally made it to an open doorway, where we were met by a receptionist. After being greeted, each of us signed a waiver form releasing the hosts from any liability and promising secrecy from all participants.

"Compliance isn't what it used to be," the dominatrix chided.

"I know, I know," was my smug reply. "I am breaking your cardinal rule—but you're the *first* person I've told this story."

"Really?"

"Absolutely!"

She gave me the look that said, "I may have been born yesterday, but not last night." I fold. "Okay, first person this month."

"That I believe."

"Besides," I rationalized, "we both know the success of those types of functions are largely dependent upon being spread by word of mouth."

"Sure. Continue."

Continue? That's it? No "please" before it or "if you would" after it. Dominate a few men, and a woman believes man's rightful place is at her feet—literally.

"Yes, ma'am," I said compliantly. She smirked, acknowledging a hint of feistiness from her playful non-sub.

I proceeded. "So, inside, I see women with their hands tied to the ceiling. Men walk by, taking turns spanking them. Another woman is over her partner's knee. He alternated between using his hands and different-sized paddles to swat her ass until it was fire-hydrant red. She screamed out in agony at first—and then apparent ecstasy!"

The corners of the dominatrix's mouth curled upward, forming a sinful smile. The idea of inflicting pain for pleasure on a willing submissive was too tantalizing. "Mm-mm," she groaned.

After noticing her obvious relish, I continued, "Now, there was equal-opportunity punishment at this party. One man, who looked like the biker from the Village People, had his hands chained to a large post. His partner stood behind him with a cat-o'-nine-tails. With each strike of the whip, the biker jumped up and down, howling at the ceiling to release his pain. This approximately 6'5", hairy-chested, handle-bar-mustache-wearing, leather-clad giant *woofed* at the whip holder seconds after each blow, signifying he was ready for another."

"Yes, that's a good slave!" she attested. "Obedience is *everything*! Have you ever thought about it?"

"About what?"

"Being a submissive?"

I laughed out loud. From her reaction, I could tell she didn't care for mine. In fact, she just stared at me.

"Oh you were serious?"

She continued waiting for a more satisfactory response, so I gave her the worded version. "No, I have *never* thought about being a submissive," I emphasized. "That type of behavior in men is equated with a pussy in my book. That entire dynamic is unnatural to me."

"Oh, but it's *natural* for a man to dominate a woman?"

"Yes, it's inherent in the title of *man*."

"That is *so* chauvinistic and so typical!"

"Precisely, true male behavior!"

She paused, looking at me with equal parts indignation and irritation. "You know something, men would be nothing without women," she said, her tone turning serious.

"We birth you into this world, nurture you throughout your lives, and for some misguided reason—you *still* think of us as the weaker sex!"

I couldn't believe I was having this conversation with a dominatrix.

"As the saying goes," she continued, "behind every good man, there is a good woman!"

"Yeah, and in your case, she is holding a whip and ball gag!"

She didn't want to but couldn't help but laugh. "You're funny! I'll have to come back some other time so we can finish this conversation."

"Any time! Meanwhile, I'll work on that wall for you. Perhaps a few heretic's forks and Spanish ticklers?"

She stopped short of the door, leaned in against the counter, and whispered, "Now you're speaking my language, honey! Get me an iron maiden and I will love you forever!" And then with a wink, she was gone.

Love hurts, all right—especially the darker shades!

JEWISH GUILT

Not long after my "session" with the dominatrix, I decided to share my experience with someone who would truly appreciate the encounter. His name was Arnie, and he was a closet submissive and huge fan of domination (male humiliation in particular). He soaked in every detail of the story with great enthusiasm and envy.

"I'm jealous, André!" he acknowledged. "I wish I had known."

"I wish I had known your whereabouts," I replied. "You're a hard man to track down."

"Well, that's true."

"Might have been a good thing you weren't here, because she doesn't strike me as the type to take kindly to an audience … as a matter of fact, I'm pretty sure she prefers one-on-one interaction."

"That's my kinda party!"

I had met Arnie through Daniel. The two had developed a close relationship over the years of Daniel working graveyard, and the dynamic between them was always rather interesting.

Arnie was nearly forty years Daniel's senior, but the age gap didn't seem to matter, as the two often enjoyed each other's company, going to breakfast after Daniel's shift at times or catching a movie on Daniel's off days.

There were, however, occasions when the two would exchange heated words and go weeks without speaking. After their last argument, I had joked with Daniel, "You and Arnie need marriage counseling."

The two did not speak during Daniel's last month with the company, yet that did not stop Arnie from periodically coming inside the store to inquire about Daniel's well-being.

"If you cared so much about Daniel, then why did you divorce him?" I ribbed Arnie.

"I'm too old and so forth to be arguing with anyone," Arnie responded, "but I wish Daniel all the best and I hope life treats him well!"

Yeah, yeah ... that's what all the divorcées say.

I never learned the cause of the rift between Daniel and Arnie, so I chalked up the split to "irreconcilable differences" and called it a relationship.

"I feel guilty about the way I let things go down with Daniel and not trying to patch things up," Arnie regretfully expressed to me one day. "Being older, I should have been the bigger person, but ... that's the way it goes sometimes."

Arnie told me that during the times he and Daniel hadn't been speaking, he would go visit the main store, where Kenneth was manager, but now, with Daniel gone, Arnie's visits to Video Expo became more and more frequent. And it was becoming obvious to me that the dynamic that had once existed between Daniel and Arnie was slowly developing, though on a lesser level, between Arnie and myself. I didn't mind, but I had no intention of going on a man-date to a darkened movie theater with Arnie. Enjoying lunch at a nearby restaurant, perhaps. And making his day with a tale about a feisty dominatrix—*why not?!*

"So André ... tell me more. Tell me more about the dominatrix! Was she cute? Was she the real deal or just a young whippersnapper?!"

I had to laugh. "*Whippersnapper?*"

So did Arnie. "Yeah! That's an old folks' term. I'm seventy-eight, you know."

"Oh, I'm familiar with the term, Arnie. I just hadn't heard it in, well— this millennium!"

"Ha-ha! See, that's the problem with you young people. You missed out on the good ole days! Our music. Our stars. Our culture. The way we lived. The way we talked."

It was hard for me, unlike Daniel, to argue with a man who bore such a close resemblance to Kris Kringle with the round red face, the swollen cheeks, the bright eyes, the wrinkles drawn perfectly by the hand of Mother Nature herself, and the iconic snow-white, curly beard. A dispute with Arnie would classify as blasphemy to a former toy-loving kid who had once looked at Santa Claus like God in an oversized red suit.

The major difference between the most famous imaginary occupant of the North Pole and Arnie lies in their lists. One rewards those who are nice, and the other prefers the naughty.

"Ooh, yeah ... hurt me, baby," Arnie cooed while looking at the cover of a bondage DVD. "I like it when they are mean and nasty!"

"And you look like such a sweet old man, Arnie!"

"Oh, I am ... that's why I like my women a bit sour!"

"If a woman enjoys running spurs across a man's scrotum or tying his penis to weighted buckets of water, she's a bit more than sour in my book!"

"She's perfect in mine!"

Well, I now knew which customer to talk to in order to get Santa a Christmas present, but she couldn't help me with what he really *needed*.

"You know, André," he told me, "I've been homeless for over twenty years, and it is time I changed that situation."

"I agree."

"It's hard to keep money when you're homeless because you have to pay for so many extra expenses."

"Like?"

"I pay $225 every month for two storage units. Any time it's late, it's $20 on top of that!"

"Damn."

"Not to mention, I have to buy already-prepared food because I have no way of cooking— and I have no place to store leftovers— unless it's something nonperishable in a box or bag."

"I can see how that would become quite costly," I said, "especially to someone on a pretty fixed income."

"Exactly!" Arnie responded. "All I get is a Social Security check and Disability check. I'm not a millionaire like Donald Trump."

"Actually, I think he's a billionaire!"

"Right! See, I don't have money like that!"

"Who does?"

"I spend a lot of time reading about the rich. Trump's father got him started in real estate—and he left him everything. Trump just kept building. He said if he had lost the presidency, he would have just gone back to building. The rich want to leave everything to their kids. That's why the poor stay poor."

"Among other reasons," I noted.

"As I was saying, for a single fella like me who is on the streets, a room wouldn't be that bad. If you go further north towards the wine country, you will get rents that are much cheaper."

"You sure about that?"

"I've heard they *do* have rooms up there. One thing I do know, I don't like San Diego! I told my brother in New York, I only like the beaches."

"C'mon, Arnie! Based on weather alone, San Diego has to provide the most ideal living situation in the country for the homeless."

"To a degree," Arnie somewhat ceded. "Maybe I'm just tired of being here and need a change of scenery. I remembered feeling this way right before I left New York."

"I know living here *has* to be easier than trying to survive on the New York streets!" I told Arnie. "The cold! *That* crowd! Those cops!"

This time in complete agreement, he said, "You're right about all those things, André. In New York, I had a cop grab my wrist, handcuff me, and say, 'Let's go!' Everyone who saw was shouting, 'Hey! What are you doing? We know him! He's not bothering anybody!'"

"He arrested you for no good reason?"

"Well, I had a small collection of pornography tapes that I used to peddle on the sidewalks and so forth, but I didn't set up in front of any of the businesses or bother anyone's customers. Someone still made a report, and that's what brought the cops out!"

"That makes more sense."

"The cop could have given me a warning or just told me to move along, though. Instead, he took me in and *left* my things there! Do you think my belongings were still there the next day when I got out?"

"I'd say they were gone in a New York minute!"

Arnie chuckled. (Yep, just like Santa!) "That's right! New York has the greatest thieves in the world. They will rob you right on the streets! I got robbed a lot! Eventually, I just kept my things in a P.O. box!"

"See, I'll bet that never happened here."

"No. Here, they just like to take things out of my shopping cart! But that is primarily my fault for leaving it unattended."

Recently, Arnie's "mobile home" had been robbed of an item of great intrinsic value. "Somebody stole my baby pictures!" he said. "Can you believe that?! I don't care about the other things they took, but those, I can't replace. I called my brother to see if he had any more copies, and unfortunately, he doesn't."

"I'm sorry to hear that, Arnie."

"Me too! I offered a reward and posted fliers around the neighborhood, but nobody has come forth yet. I tell you, the more I have to be around people, the more I'd rather have a dog!"

"Don't get a Chihuahua!"

"Ha-ha! You don't care for those, eh?"

"No."

"You know what the worst part about it is, André?"

"What?"

"People steal from me, but I still help others out when they ask me. I feel guilty if I have something and someone else needs it!"

"You've really got that guilt thing working, don't you, Arnie?"

"What can I say—I'm Jewish!"

"Is that what it is?"

"I don't know. That's just the way I am. Always trying to help. Always trying to fix things."

"It can be a real curse, I know!"

"You should have seen me during 9/11!"

"The terrorist attacks?"

"Yes."

"You were there?" "Yes."

Arnie took a moment to collect his thoughts. The memories from that day, of course, were not pleasant ones. "André ... there was so much screaming!" he recalled.

"So many tears."

"There were thick clouds of smoke for blocks and blocks. The heat and debris in the air burned your eyes! People were choking, gagging, crying. ... I've never seen anything like it!"

Arnie mumbled a few indiscernible words. The anguished look on his face provided a glimpse into the distress and destruction of that day. That twinkle in his eye reminiscent of Jolly Old Saint Nicholas was now dimmed by one of the darkest days in our country's history.

It was time to change the subject.

"So Arnie, a guy brought in a bunch of classic movies the other day!"

He perked up.

"Oh yeah?!"

I knew that would do the trick! Second only to Arnie's obsession with domination is his love for the older porn starlets from the seventies and eighties. And since I was in the gift-giving mood, I decided to throw in a bonus. I reached underneath the counter, grabbed a manila envelope, and handed it to Arnie. "Here, open this!"

He did as instructed, pulling out a single sheet of paper. The sparkle returned as he gazed upon a list of all the top porn stars from their respective decades.

"Ooh, André ... where did you get this?"

"Wikipedia."

"That Internet is something else, I tell you. I need to get a better phone. I'll have to bring you something the next time I see you."

"That won't be necessary, Arnie. It's a gift!"

"Oh, I have to!"

"No, you don't."

"Are you sure?"

"I'm positive."

Arnie's excitement rivaled that of any kid on Christmas Day. "Amazing!" he marveled. "These are household names. Back in New York, I used to sell a lot of their tapes for food and/or money. They helped me to survive."

"I'm sure they would be happy to know their work served a greater purpose, Arnie."

"Yeah, survival is pretty important. I used to follow the careers of some of my favorites. That always helped me to keep my mind off my situation when things got really bad!"

"Who are some of your favorites?"

"Well, let's see here, André ... Erica Boyer. Georgina Spelvin. Gloria Leonard. Marilyn Chambers. Sharon Mitchell."

"You know, Erica Boyer passed away not that long ago," I mentioned.

"Yes, I was very sad to hear that," Arnie indicated.

"Me too! She was one of the first women I ever saw in an adult film."

Arnie was so enthralled by the names on the list that he didn't even hear my statement.

One performer made him stop and take pause. "Now she is the best ever!" he boasted. "My all-time favorite!"

There could be only one person to whom Arnie was referring.

"Nina Hartley!" he swooned. "Now she has it all! Class. Beauty. Brains."

"And she still has a killer body!" I added. "Tight. Toned. Ripped. I remember in the eighties thinking she was a fitness model or something. And she had 'junk in the trunk' back when white women in the biz weren't known for their derrieres!"

"You're right, André. I read somewhere that said after a short time in the business, Nina's buttocks quickly became her trademark."

"Yup!"

"Did you know she used to be a registered nurse?"

"Yes, I did."

"But did you know she graduated magna cum laude in her class?"

"No, but it doesn't surprise me, considering what she's been doing over the last ten years."

"You mean pornography or otherwise?"

"Both, actually! I read that she has long been the actress called upon to be the articulate female voice in defense of the adult film industry's right to exist. And most of her recent work involves instructional videos about sexual intercourse—of course—as well as foreplay, anal sex, and even bondage!" [12] There was that word again.

"Oh?!" Arnie yelped. "Bondage—really?"

"Yes, Arnie—really!"

"Would you happen to have a copy of her bondage DVD?"

"Not at the moment, but I'm sure I can order it for the store."

---

[12] Wikipedia, The Free Encyclopedia, https://en.wikipedia.org/wiki/Nina_Hartley

Arnie smiled and his face pruned even more, the wrinkles seeming to multiply. "I'd really appreciate that," he said. "I'd really like to get my hands on that ... and I could play it on my portable DVD player whenever I wanted."

"There you go."

"André, around how much would that cost me?"

"It would be regular price, which is $39.99, but for you, we'll work something out."

"If you can do that, I will get you anything you want—name your price!"

"Arnie, we've been over this; I don't want anything."

"I know, but I can't just accept your generosity without returning the favor. I would feel ..."

"Guilty?"

TALE OF THE TAPE

Thanks to a new city ordinance—and much to the chagrin of our former night crowd—there was no more graveyard shift. Thirty years of twenty-four-hour service were gone within a week. Our new store hours would be from seven a.m. until two a.m. ... and I was just starting to like them.

On the first Monday and Tuesday mornings, I arrived right before seven o' clock, opening the store to a sanctuary of peace and tranquility. I was alone for a solid twenty minutes before any human interaction. It was *so* refreshing, a great start to the week! But, as I've said before, good times never last long.

On Wednesday, I was in the store about two minutes before my first customer came knocking. On Thursday, we were all arriving at the same time. By Friday, they were camped out in the parking lot waiting for me—along with their complaints. "It says on the website you guys are twenty-four hours," one shouted. "You should change that!"

I looked over my shoulder and scowled at him, and he took a step backward. "I'll be sure to relay that to the owner," I scoffed.

"Man, I didn't even know you guys changed your hours," another chirped as I entered the store. "I'm off to Vegas and I need to pick up some movies for the bachelor party."

The last thing I wanted to hear this early morning was how much fun someone was about to go have in Vegas while I was working, waiting eight hours for my weekend to begin, but I didn't want to be a Debbie downer, so I gently apprised him of the situation. "Well, sir, unfortunately, you're going to have to wait a few minutes while I get things ready inside the store."

He pointed at the door and moaned, "Aww, don't you guys open at seven?"

I stopped worrying about being a Debbie downer at this point. It now took everything in me to refrain from being a dick! Sarcasm is my usual weapon of choice in these situations, but because he wanted to be factual, I decided to terminate the conversation via a technicality. I looked back at him. "You know what? You're right! We do open at seven, and since it's only 6:55, I guess that means I'll see you in five minutes!"

With that, I closed the door and promptly locked it behind me. I could see his sad puppy dog eyes peeping through the door, reminiscent of the last pooch at a pet adoption, his hot breath spreading across the glass. I'd still managed to be a dick, but oh well—I prefer cats.

I redeemed myself somewhat by not making Scruffy wait long. It took me only a few minutes, as I'd told him, to prepare the drawer, and once that was done, I unlocked the door and put him out of his misery.

"Hey thanks, I'm *really* in a hurry!" he told me.

Turning my head, I mumbled, "Yeah, whatever."

While he riffled through the box covers in the amateur section, my buddy Dorian came into the store to return some movies. Dorian was about ten years younger than me, but the full beard he sported a la Abraham Lincoln made him appear to be ten years older. He wore a stocking cap on his head, and his long, thick braids draped across his shoulders and hung down to the middle of his back.

In the shop, a clerk and regular generally have specific topics they cover whenever they see each other. Banter between Dorian and me often centered around sports, with both of us sharing an athletic background.

"You look tired," I observed. "Did you just get off work?"

"Yeah, man. I jus' dropped by to return deez rentals, and then I gotta go scoop up mah son!"

Dorian worked the graveyard shift at the local grocery store. He labeled and stocked products as well as drove a forklift. "So when did y'all get deez new hours?"

"Oh, about a week ago."

"You like 'em?"

"I did for about two days. The customers were a bit thrown off at first but, they seem to have adjusted to the change."

Speaking of thrown off—here came Scruffy with two movies in hand. "All right, man, I'll take these, and then I'm gone." I pulled his selections, bagged them, rang him up, and sent the puppy off to play, his tail in full wag. "Thanks, man! We are going to have so much fun. I can't wait!"

Once he left, Dorian asked, "Where dat dude goin'? He ran outta here like he stole sumthin'!"

"Oh, he's got a weekend of double Ds and debauchery awaiting him in Vegas."

While sorting through movies, Dorian came across a familiar face. "Hey, I know dis chick! We went to school together back in da day. I tried to holla at her for a lil while, but she was too much work!" Translation: She wasn't easy! "Now she gettin' paid for her work!"

"I've had a few girls come in here trying to find their movies," I said.

"For reals?"

"Yeah."

"Anybody good?"

"Julia Bond came through once with a few of her friends."

"Was she wit a gang of hotties?!" Dorian wondered.

"Nah," I replied, bursting his bubble. "A couple of girlfriends and a gay male."

"It trips me out dat sum of these girls wud even do dis stuff. I mean, everybody gonna see it and know it's dem!"

"Well, with girls like your friend, I think it's the allure of fast, easy money. Their intention was to be in a couple movies, make a quick thousand dollars, and be out. Others got smart and started making their own movies to become known or starting their own websites altogether!"

"You right 'bout dat. Nowadays, it seems like everybody got a tape."

"Yup! Thanks to cell phones, camcorders, and the Internet. Now it's all about hits and views!"

"Man, how'd all dis shit start?"

I didn't know if Dorian's question was more rhetorical than actually requiring an answer, but I gave one anyway.

I told him I believed it had all started back in 1984 at the MTV Video Music Awards with Madonna's live performance of her hit song "Like a Virgin," which ushered in the start of women successfully marketing themselves and profiting from so-called sexual exploitation.

In masterful fashion, Madonna had used the image of a virgin bride writhing around on stage in her wedding dress to spark the type of controversy that would help fuel her thirty-plus-year musical career. Today, other female entertainers such as Rihanna, Lady Gaga, Beyoncé, and Miley Cyrus have learned to replicate that formula to varying degrees of success.

Porn is no different. When Pamela Anderson and Tommy Lee's sex tape first exploded onto the adult scene over twenty years ago, it was thought to be a bad thing for the infamous Hollywood couple, but in fact, just the opposite proved to be true as the famous vacation footage served to boost Anderson's sex-goddess image to Marilyn Monroe-like status—in addition to cementing Lee's reputation as the ultimate rocker and bad boy.

Many a sex tape would follow once celebrities realized this was the ideal way to increase public sex appeal, which directly correlated with an increase in appearances, sponsorships, and, ultimately, money!

Paris Hilton—whose footage looks like something filmed through night goggles during Operation Desert Storm—Kendra Wilkinson, Montana Fishburne, and Teen Mom Farrah Abraham (two tapes) are among the other more notable celebrities to have sex tapes on the market. None have profited and benefited more from this phenomenon than Kim Kardashian, however. In the beginning, she was simply the daughter of Robert Kardashian.

Then she became known as Ray J's lover, next as Reggie Bush's girlfriend and until recently, the wife of Kanye West. But through it all, Kim's career (expertly managed by mother Kris Jenner) has blossomed beyond expectation. Her popularity is no longer the result of a male association, not bad for someone who has been tagged as being famous for simply being famous. She has modeling gigs, clothing and beauty lines, a possible career in law, and one of the most popular reality television shows (*Keeping Up With The Kardashians*) of all time- notoriety all launched by a 2007 sex tape with Ray J.

Madonna laid the blueprint that other women have learned to follow: If you're going to be sexually exploited, do it yourself! That way, the female takes power away from the male, who is traditionally attempting to exploit her. Madonna best exemplified this when *Playboy* magazine released nude photographs—which they did not shoot—of the singer before she became famous. When the pictures came out, Madonna, instead of panicking and lashing out, was completely honest about the situation, stating she had needed the money and had no regrets.

A possible public-relations disaster turned into a celebration of Madonna as a straight-shooting, determined, savvy businesswoman who would do whatever it took to be successful.

She realized—and cleverly used to her advantage—the fact that women are truly the powerful ones in the sexual arena. This is especially true for porn, which is why females, not men, are usually featured on the hetero box covers: Men want to see women, *and* women want to see women.

"Never really thought 'bout Madonna like dat," Dorian admitted. "She a boss!"

"Yup! Even Jay Z paid homage when he referred to himself as the male Madonna in his song 'Unbreakable.'"

These days, photographing oneself with a camera phone (taking selfies) and posting the pictures on social media sites is the in thing.

Selfies have become the new amateur porn, as the goal apparently is to show as much tits and ass as possible—and the bigger the better.

"Pretty soon, all deez movies won't even be necessary. We can get it off the Internet faster and cheaper."

"That's true. But there is something taboo about watching a tape. Perhaps it's the perception of peeping in on someone performing a very private act. That, in a nutshell, explains pornography's popularity and resulting success: Take what is forbidden and make it for profit!"

LESBIFRIENDS

The phone rang.

André: Video Expo, this is André speaking. How may I help you?

Caller (female voice): Yes, I have a charge here on my credit card for a dildo!

André: Okay. And ...

Caller: *And* I have never been to your store!

Uh-oh! Somebody's in trouble.

André: Well, does anyone else have access to your credit card?

Caller: My husband!

Big trouble!

Caller: The bastard hasn't brought anything new home to me, though!

André: Well, ma'am, ... I'm not sure I know what you want me to do ...

Caller: If you ever see him in that store again, tell him to go *fuck* himself with that dildo!

André: Ma'am, I have no idea who you are even talking about!

Caller: Are you covering up for him?

André: Excuse me?

Caller: You men are *always* covering up for each other! He's probably in that store all the time! In fact, he's probably in there with his little whore *right now*!

André: I wouldn't know anything about that.

Caller: Don't play stupid!

No, this bitch did not just call me stupid!

Caller: Let me speak to the manager! I'll bet he's seen them together!

God, why Friday?! Couldn't her credit card statement have come the next day? Dealing with pissed off, jilted, issue-laden significant others is usually a Monday or Tuesday thing, but my last working day before the weekend? Oh well, Dré, just get it over with. *And who the fuck is she calling stupid?!*

André: I'm the manager.

Caller: See! You know the bastard, *don't you?* You know all those people that come in that store and what they are up to!

André: Actually, I don't …

Caller: How could you work in a place like that?!

Here we go.

André: Listen, ma'am …

Caller: Stop calling me ma'am, I'm not a fuckin' old lady!

André: Look! I'm just trying to be polite! You don't need to speak to me like that!

Caller: *Oh*, I am so sorry! Have I offended you? Are you upset now too?

André: Upset wouldn't be the word, but I could pretend to be if it would make *you* feel better!

Caller: *Oh*, like you are pretending not to know my husband!

That backfired.

André: Listen, ma'am, err, miss, I understand you are upset, but …

Caller: How could you possibly understand? Do you have a cheating no-good son of a bitch for a husband running around town with his little whore?

André: Can't say I do.

Caller: Then don't try and empathize with me.

André: Actually, I was sympathizing …

Caller: Whatever! You tell him to keep his whore, because he is a lousy fuck anyway! That's why I have a girlfriend!

Click.

Two days later, a male customer walked up to the counter.

André: May I help you?

Customer: Do you know if any of your movies have copy-guards?

André: You're not supposed to copy any of the movies and try to resell them.

Customer: I know. I have no intentions of selling them. I want to be able to edit them.

André: Edit them? For what purpose?

Customer: To watch! I only like to see women—no men.

André: Then why not just watch lesbian movies and save yourself the trouble?

Customer: I don't buy lesbian movies because they usually don't have the big-name stars and new starlets in them.

André: So you want to see women, not men, and you buy straight movies? What, you edit out the sex scenes or something?

Customer: Yes! I edit out the footage of men and splice together the shots of the females.

André: And you have equipment that does this?

Customer: Yes, but if it says 'No Regional Coding' on the box, then I can't do it.

André: What does that mean, exactly?

Customer: Basically, it means the footage cannot be recorded and edited.

André: In all my years of working for this company, I don't think I have ever heard of that before.

Customer: Well, it used to be where you could record movies with no problem. Then due to all the piracy, they started copy-guarding.

André: And how does that work?

Customer: Basically, if someone is trying to record a DVD, the disc sends out an electronic signal that will either scramble the picture or shut off the recorder.

André: You learn something new every day.

Customer: I figure if I am going to spend money on a DVD, I may as well see something I want to watch—and that's *women*!

"If only we could solve the whole 'male problem' that simply," Anna wished after I repeated these conversations to her a few weeks later. "Replace 'em or completely edit 'em out of the picture *altogether!*"

"I didn't realize we had a 'male problem,'" I replied.

"That's because you're a man!"

Zing!

Anna is a former customer with whom I developed a close friendship over the years. We enjoy getting together at her apartment from time to time to engage in a bit of intellectual discourse—or verbal sparring. Both are fun.

She holds very strong feminist views (in case you couldn't tell) and is a lesbian (in case you couldn't tell)—and a hot one! Lipstick to the core. Five-foot-four inches and 120 pounds of feisty redhead. (What a waste!)

"So, Anna, you are implying I am either out of touch or in denial—neither of which is very flattering!"

"Less out of touch, more in denial. It's not your fault, though. All men are! It's a flaw in your way of thinking."

"Could the flaw possibly be in your logic?"

"Of course not!"

"Of course not! And what *exactly* are men in denial about?"

Anna folded her arms and crossed her legs. "Your importance in society! Men overvalue themselves. They think women can't function without them."

"I suppose, Anna, the world is in shambles right now because of men, right?"

"*You* said it! And whenever we get our first female president, she is going to prove it!"

"Oh God!" I mumbled under my breath.

"*Goddess!*" she corrected me.

"God is a female now?! Since when?"

"Since *always*! Why does *she* have to be male?"

"Why does *he* have to be female?"

She then went biblical on me. "God is also referred to as *The Creator*, correct?"

"Yes, that is one of *his* aliases."

"Okay, then think about it. ... The *female* is the one who physically ushers a spirit into this life."

"They don't *create* the life," I reminded her. "That egg doesn't fertilize itself!"

She smiled and looked upon me triumphantly, as if she had just conquered all of mankind for womankind's sake. "See, there is that overvaluing. You men are simply *sperm donors!*"

I too could play this game. "Oh, okay ... so thinking along those lines, that means women are basically *incubators?*"

"There would be no repopulating of the planet if it weren't for us!" Anna boasted.

This intellectual discourse was fast becoming a verbal-sparring session. She had led with a jab, so I countered with one of my own. It was my turn to get biblical. "If that's the *case*, Anna, why then in the Bible does it talk about man going forth to spread his seed to replenish the earth?"

Seemingly before my punch had even landed, she had sidestepped the blow and loaded up the overhand right. "First off, the Bible is written by men, so everything is slanted," she countered. "Second, that seed needs *fertile ground* to grow!"

I took that first hit on the chin, having no real defense. I managed to deflect the second blow, though, well enough to strike back. "Rich fertile ground or dry barren desert, nothing grows without a *seed*!"

I was used to having such exchanges with men—not on this topic, of course—and sometimes even with women, but in a more spirited tone. Going toe to toe with Anna was different. This lesbian was a different breed of fighter, combining the passion and cunning of a female with a man's steely resolve. Definite edge.

Early in the bout, we'd used religion as our fighting platform and had reached a stalemate. Anna looked to gain an advantage in the later rounds by using her secret weapon: sex. She pressed forward, cornering me. "If God is a man ... why would he make it so you guys can only have one orgasm but women can have *multiple*?"

Caught right on the chin again! This time, I slid down the ropes, falling to a knee before dropping to the canvas. The basest argument for proving God is a woman was the one that most struck a chord with me. Yeah I know, I'm a guy ... but it is something to ponder!

I thought back to my time with a former girlfriend who could experience as many orgasms as I could serve up. I had always taken pride in making a woman cum—an ego thing— and I had been with women who had multiple orgasms before, but this girlfriend could have multiple *multiple* orgasms. One time, I stopped counting at *eight*! By the time I had reached that same number, three or four days later, she had already reached the double digits. No fair!

The fight was over. I just laid there on my back while being counted out. I was staring at ceiling lights, nothing left in the reserve tank. No rebuttal. Anna knew it, too. "Don't have an answer for that one, Dré, do you?" she gloated. "God knew what *she* was doing!"

She then switched roles to that of gracious host and went into the kitchen to make margaritas. As I stirred around the living room, licking my wounds, someone pounded on the front door. "Get that!" Anna screamed over the roar of the blender.

I hadn't known she was expecting company, but once I opened the door, I certainly didn't mind! Standing before me was what I would call a *goddess*! She was six feet tall (five feet of that seeming to be legs), with flowing brown hair, emerald-green eyes, and a body that must have been the result of a *Weird Science* experiment.

"Hello," she mouthed to me. It was like she didn't actually speak the word but *breathed* it and air currents floated it past my ears.

The cat must have been holding my tongue with a vise grip, because the only response I could muster was that stupid smile— more like a smirk—that guys have on their faces when the brain temporarily shuts down.

Anna returned from the kitchen holding drinks. She broke the awkward silence—which seemed to last an eternity—with welcomed words. "Oh, I see you have met my girlfriend."

"Uh … yeah, I sure have," I finally uttered.

"Well, are you two going to just stand there and guard the door or *actually* come inside the living room and sit down?"

The goddess gracefully walked past me and reached out to Anna, grabbing her by the waist. She pulled Anna close. Anna collapsed into her arms, and the two began kissing passionately.

Many a hetero male would wait a lifetime to witness two gorgeous lipsticks making out right in front of him, especially with lesbian consent! I never saw it that way, though. To me, it was no more than a tease! I couldn't participate, so what's to get excited about? It's like being on the Mercedes-Benz showroom floor with Honda money. It's like waiting on the sidelines for the chance to play in the big game but never getting the opportunity. It's like when Charlie Brown charges to kick the football, foolishly thinking this time Lucy is not going to swipe it away … and at the last minute, she does just that and he ends up falling flat on his back. *Again.* This was partial gift, mostly curse! This was *forbidden fruit*!

"Ahem," I said, clearing my throat. "I think those drinks are starting to get *warm*."

Anna, blushing, slightly pulled away from her partner. "Oh, I'm sorry, Dré. I got a bit pre-occupied."

"Didn't notice."

"Let me formally introduce you two. Samantha, this is André … Dré, Samantha."

The goddess, now identified, smiled at me. "Nice to meet you, André."

"The pleasure is mine, Samantha."

"I bet it is," Anna goaded. "It's not every day a guy gets to see two hot women making out in front of him!"

Damn, are lesbians mind readers, too?!

"Oh! That's right, André. I forgot. You're probably used to seeing stuff like this all the time where you work."

"Really?" Samantha said, intrigued. "Where does he work?"

Way to put me on the spot, Anna! Generally, I like to ease into the subject of my employment. It can be a polarizing topic of conversation, so I never know what kind of reaction I will get. But since Anna put it out there, I revealed, "I manage a porn shop," much to Samantha's delight.

"Wow, really? I bet you have some stories to tell!"

Sensing an opening, I glanced at Anna. "You have no idea, Samantha. Ever heard the one about how Anna and I met?"

Sensing trouble, Anna glared at me and quickly tried to change the subject. "Hey, these margaritas aren't going to drink themselves! He can bore you with that story some other time."

Now it was my turn to provoke. "Anna, you know none of my stories are boring—*especially* yours!"

When I first met Anna at the store, she was dating several girls—a fact I would come to learn later as we became friends. Samantha was one of the many, but not the one Anna was going to visit that night with a brand-new vibrator—a fact that Anna certainly wanted to remain hidden, as evidenced by her shaking her head at me while extending a margarita—her peace offering.

"It's great when you can win a fight without landing a single punch," I bragged. "You know what I mean, Samantha?"

Anna crossed her eyes and grunted, "I *really* hope you like that margarita!"

Proud of my redemption, I plopped down on the couch. "Best I ever had, Anna. Thanks!"

Samantha, still somewhat puzzled, joined Anna on the opposite sofa. "So what did I miss before I arrived?"

"Well, Samantha, your *girlfriend* here believes men overvalue their importance in society." Samantha turned to Anna and smiled. "Absolutely, they do!"

Another one? Was Anna's "lone-nut" theory (my categorization) in fact a popular belief held by lesbians at large, even though Samantha operated under obvious bias? Samantha then said something that struck a little too close to home. "Besides, who needs a man? ... We have vibrators."

Déjà vu!

My mind went back to that television special about the history of the vibrator. Those, however, had been opinions given by so-called experts. I was about to get the scoop straight from the lesbians' vaginas—err, mouth.

"See, we have gotten the 'business' of sex out of the way by eliminating all of man's sweet talking and lies," Samantha said. "Now women have found a way to maximize the pleasure while eliminating the heartache that can come along with it."

"Yeah, just think of a vibrator purchase as lesbian circumcision," Anna added. "We take away the best part of the man …"

"And leave behind all the bullshit!" Samantha finished.

They laughed. Snuggled. Kissed. Pawed at each other. Their exuberant show of unbridled passion and uncontrollable giggles was a shameless mockery of me and my kind. But what if this was woman's diabolical scheme to eradicate man from the sexual landscape? Women don't need to have sex with men to have babies. They can use a sperm donor, as Anna had so kindly reminded me. Women weren't cutting out the middle man; they were simply cutting out the middle—and totally disregarding the man!

I tried a gentler approach to convince these scourges of men that we are not just sexual objects. *I can't believe I just thought that!* "You know, we are more than just a cock and balls," I insisted. *Delicate, right?*

They locked arms in preparation for their tag-team male bash. "André, women are generally better listeners, are more sensitive, and are more understanding than men," Anna claimed.

Samantha sat beside Anna, lovingly playing with her partner's hair. "Don't forget we are also more forgiving, sweetheart!"

"Oh please!" I objected. "When a woman gets upset, she isn't listening to a word that is being said. And we won't even talk about holding a grudge! As far as forgiving, here's a little story for you." I went on about how a woman had once come into the store and told me that she had just dumped her boyfriend, whom she had caught cheating.

The lady had said to me that the best way to get over an old guy is to "get under a new one."

"Right concept, wrong gender!" Anna interrupted as the ladies laughed.

I continued to talk about this woman's breakup "rules," which she said apply to most women. The first is to get a new hairdo. This, she said, is like "shedding skin" and separating from the past. The second is to go out to the club and get plenty of attention to feel sexy. The third is to make anyone around them who is "too happy" feel miserable because that's how she's feeling.

"Ha, *that's* your example?" Anna scoffed.

"Dré, I can see the first two, but the third one?"

"All I know is she was one of *yours*."

"All I know is you've met some pretty shallow women."

"Can't argue that point. But that doesn't mean what she said isn't true. Besides, I could say you've met some pretty shallow men—which some guys would argue is the reason why you've turned to a woman for companionship."

"Valid point," Samantha acknowledged. "A guy once said to me I must have been hurt pretty bad by some man to love vagina and hate penis!"

Anna huffed and sipped on her margarita. "That guy is an idiot!" She then pressed the glass to Samantha's lips. Her lover tilted her head back and downed its remaining contents.

They both looked at me. I returned a blank stare, awaiting their final assault.

"You see, *that* is the popular misconception about lesbians," Anna began. "We don't hate penis …"

Again, Samantha finished. "We just don't care for the skin attached to it!"

They laughed. Snuggled. Kissed. Pawed at each other. A shameless mockery.

SUCKER FOR LOVE

Another day, another lube-soaked dollar.

Sal was in the back of the store, collecting money out of the booths. I was sitting up front, rocking back and forth in my reclining chair and staring out at hundreds of topless women. Breasts of all shapes and sizes: boulders, bee stings, beanbags, bullets, bazookas, buttons, cantaloupes, cupcakes, gumdrops, honeydews, flappers, jawbreakers, niblets, num-nums, polygons, pokers, sandbags, spheres, tidbits, tooters, and of course—*whoppers!*

I was in mammary heaven, mentally motorboating between clouds of cleavage. I was so preoccupied that it took a moment to realize a customer had walked through the door. (Or perhaps I just didn't care!) "Dream job, eh?!" He whispered in passing.

"Ya think so?" I responded. Then I thought, *You know what? That is quite an accurate description.* Starting off, you can't believe that you come to work every day and are surrounded by pictures and videos of some of the most beautiful and sexy women in the world. Later on, you can't believe that you come to work every day and become involved in situations of such intrigue, indiscretion—and idiocy!

It *is* a dream!

Sal emerged from the back, the money bag swollen to capacity. "Hey, André! How was your weekend?"

"It was good, Sal! But it looks like the store had a better one!"

"Yeah, *this* store did pretty good. Certainly better than the stores up north."

"Oh?"

"I was up in the Salinas area on Saturday, and they were hardly making any money, but that had more to do with the manager than anything else!"

"Really? What was going on—if I might ask?"

"What *wasn't* going on is the better question!"

"This sounds good!"

Sal pulled the shift envelopes out of the safe and dumped them onto the counter. He expertly sorted through the mess while recapping the weekend's events. "Let's see—to begin with, the manager was stealing," Sal revealed. "He oversees three stores up there and he collects all the money each morning. Before going to the bank to put the money in the company's account, he was taking what he wanted out of the envelopes and only reporting what was left."

"Wow!"

"It gets even better!"

"Okay …"

"The store he works in has arcades with live girls behind the glass … are you familiar?"

"Yes."

"Well, when he first became manager about six months ago, we warned him not to get involved with any of the dancers."

Speaking from my own personal experience, that's easier said than done! But one thing I have always managed to steer clear of is dating at the workplace. "Fishing off the company pier seems to always lead to trouble," I said. "The fact that it involves an exotic dancer makes it even worse!"

"We warned him, André! He fucked around and caught a barracuda! None of the employees or other dancers like her because she is a bitch! And believe it or not, that still isn't the best part!"

"This is a bit much for a Monday morning!"

"He got the girl pregnant—*and* he has a wife and kids at home!"

"You gotta be kidding me!"

"Couldn't make this shit up if I tried!"

"Sal, how does that happen when you work in a store full of condoms?"

He laughed. "I don't know, but he is in real trouble now, because the dancer has kids too!"

"It's still getting better!"

"He's going to lose one family and, I guess, gain another."

"Yeah, but it sounds like he's losing value on the trade-in!"

We both laughed and then said our good-byes. Sal headed back to the main office and me back to my comfy chair, but my plans of making a return trip to dreamland were canceled by a phone call. It was Kenneth. "Hey, André! What's goin' on?"

"Not too much, Kenneth! I hear all the excitement is taking place up north!"

"I know, right? The shit is crazy!"

"So, what's up?"

"I'm letting you know that you are going to have a trainee today!"

"Oh, okay. Cool!"

As manager of the main store, Kenneth always gets a crack at training the new hires first. His shop is big, beautiful, and full of the latest and greatest in high-priced adult novelties. The atmosphere is warm and inviting, the spacious parking lot often littered with expensive automobiles belonging to classy clientele.

Basically, his store is everything Video Expo is not—but our store is the *true* training ground! My fellow managers and peers have dubbed it the Jungle—and for good reason. The crazies abound. Lunacy at every turn. Disorder only a booth away. This is where trainees are sent to gain exposure to the flip side of adult retail. This is where trainees are sent to see if they are serious about a clerking job in our company. This is where we "make 'em or break 'em!" So, after Kenneth has spent a day or two with a potential clerk, he calls and lets me know that the trainee is coming my way—and what the latest odds are on them returning the next day!

"The guy coming is a roommate of a former employee who worked for us for several years," Kenneth said. "I'm sure he has heard all the stories and knows what he may potentially be getting himself into."

"Well, we'll see when he gets here!"

"Exactly! He's scheduled to start at two o' clock."

"Okay, I'll be sure to roll out the red carpet."

"You're going to take him back to the booths so he can meet the usual suspects?"

"Yup!"

"He's done!"

I laughed before hanging up the phone. Little did I know that the joke was on me!

Sure enough, around 1:50 p.m., a man I had never seen before came through the door and cautiously stopped at the edge of the counter. It was him. Even if Kenneth hadn't called and told me I was getting a trainee—as has happened in the past—I'd still know he was new.

Talk about sticking out like a sore thumb! He had that "freshman face" new kids wear on the first day of high school: the overwhelmed look in the eyes that always gives innocence away. I removed the awkwardness from the situation by extending a greeting and asking, "Are you here to train?"

"Yes, yes, I am!" he stuttered. "I'm Billy, Billy Love. But most people call me by my family-given nickname, Buddy."

Buddy Love? Seriously? You don't look like Sherman Klump's evil alter ego. Courtney Love was the only person I could think of with that last name, and if he was anything like her, well ... he'd fit right in!

I gestured for my new trainee to join me behind the counter. "Come on back ... Billy."

Billy was a pudgy fellow, square-jawed with short black hair and brown eyes. As he removed his windbreaker, I noticed his arms and neck were covered with ink! His shirt read, "Real Men Wear Tats!" I guess Billy was a Love(r) *and* a fighter! I extend my hand and shook his. "My name is André! I'm the manager."

"Nice to meet you, André." Firm grip. (I would learn how he got it that way very soon.)

After the exchange of pleasantries, I showed Billy where the time cards were located and demonstrated how to punch in on the clock. He still had a few minutes remaining before starting work and chose to spend them inspecting some of the products—little mini vibes, in particular.

"These look like candy," Billy commented. "I noticed them when I was training in the other store." The vibrators come in a box of thirty, colors varying between blue, red, yellow, and green. I didn't know what candy Billy was being reminded of, but I went with it. "Yeah, I guess they kinda do. But the only actual candy we have in the store are the Edible Undies—and Pecker Suckers."

"Pecker Suckers?!"

"Yeah, Pecker Suckers."

"Where?"

"They're at the end of the counter in that little plastic fishbowl."

Pecker Suckers are ... pretty self-explanatory, but for those of you who are not visual thinkers or who are really just that naïve, imagine a mold of a cock and balls made of candy impaled on a little white stick. What flavors, you wonder? Strawberry, orange, and cherry.

The suckers are popular party favors amongst the bachelorette crowd, along with the Edible Undies, Blow-Me Dice, and naked-firemen playing cards. Sometimes guys even buy them as gag gifts to get a laugh out of their girlfriends or when playing a joke on a soon-to-be-married pal, so when Billy began closely inspecting the confectionery delights, I thought nothing of it. Not even after I heard him say, "I'm hungry."

The clock finally struck 2:00 p.m., and it was time for training. Billy clocked in and asked, "Before we get started, do you mind if I buy one of these suckers?"

"Not at all."

So he did. And I put away the miscellaneous papers scattered on the counter in preparation for our walk around.

"Okay, André, I'm ready!"

At least one of us was prepared for what was about to happen!

I started my orientation with the DVD players be-cause clerks spend a good portion of the day operating these machines. "Billy, I know the other store has a computer where you can click on the mouse to switch between the various players, but here, you have to do it manually."

No response, save the faint sound of paper crinkling.

"Billy, here to the right you will find all of the discounted DVDs that I have marked down. They range anywhere from $9.99 to $19.99. The higher-priced DVDs are further down the wall." At this time, Billy was standing over my shoulder. Suddenly, I got a whiff of something sweet. It smelled like strawberry.

I thought, If I ever dreamt on the job, please let it be now! But, unfortunately, reality was standing right beside me, pinching my arm. (More like slurping in my ear!) I did everything I could to keep from looking at Billy. As long as he was at my back, I wouldn't have to witness a grown man slobbering all over a candy penis! *Vigorously*, from the sound of it.

"These are really good, André! Have you ever tried one?"

Refusing to turn around, I responded, "No, Billy, can't say that I have." Like any true professional—or mildly disturbed heterosexual—I sharpened my focus on the task at hand and continued with my training. "Here are the high-end DVDs I was telling you about, along with the box sets and disc sets."

"So I have a question, André."

"What might that be, Billy?"

"You see *this*?"

"What is it?"

"I don't know. I saw it at the other store and forgot to ask. Perhaps you can tell me." Initially, it seemed that I had one of two choices: to be rude (if I didn't turn around) or repulsed (if I did). Then I remembered I knew every product in my store! All I needed was a simple description, so turning to face him wouldn't be necessary. In fact, providing him with an answer in this manner may come off as impressive instead of impolite.

"Describe it to me, Billy."

"It's a little white box that has a portrait of an old Chinese man with Chinese writing underneath him. On the label, it says, 'China Brush.'

What's that?" I was surprised Billy had stopped enjoying his sucker long enough to say all that. (For him, that was a mouthful of a different sort.)

"That's a numbing cream," I informed him. "Guys put it on the end of their penis to dull the sensitivity and keep from ejaculating too quickly."

"Huh, interesting."

That he found interesting?

"Wow!" Billy marveled. "You really know your stuff!"

Mission accomplished. Now, I wished Billy would accomplish his mission and finish off that damn sucker! But that was going to take a while, judging by the way he was savoring his treat—a fact not lost on a lustful pair of eyes in the distance. (Yes, Billy had an audience!)

When I finally turned around, Billy now having his back to me, I noticed a customer peeking his head around the corner. One couldn't help but notice the salacious grin on his face—except for Billy, of course, who was totally oblivious, lost in his lollicock, err, pop. Billy took a seat in the chair, swiveled in my direction, and started asking more questions. Avoiding eye contact would be much more difficult this time.

Now face to face with Billy, I employed a tactic that speakers are encouraged to use when nervous and speaking in front of a large audience. No, I didn't picture him naked. I picked a spot on his tattooed arm and focused on it while answering him. I figured this way, he would think I was simply admiring his artwork.

My aversion technique worked only briefly, because I ran into a couple of problems, the first being that the human eye has this thing called peripheral vision! The second being that the human mind has this thing called curiosity! Both got the best of me—you know, like when you're driving down the freeway and all signs point to an accident: heavy traffic ahead, smoke, possibly fire, police cars, an ambulance. The car wreck is clear on the other side of the divider, but all the looky-loos in front of you have to slow down to check it out, even though there is absolutely nothing they can do about it! You curse, scream, perhaps throw your hands up, while waiting in traffic. And of course, what do *you* do the minute you drive by the scene of the wreck? Uh-huh. Seeing is believing—well, in most cases, because I couldn't believe what I was seeing! I remained a doubting Thomas even though I had indisputable, irrefutable proof.

Then it became obvious: I didn't want to believe it, because that would involve admitting that I was actually standing there, watching another man expertly tongue-polishing the balls on a Pecker Sucker; ramming the thing in and out of his mouth; slurping, slobbering, and salivating, working it like a bomb pop fresh off the ice-cream truck on a midsummer day at high noon!

In the adult biz, another term for fellatio is playing the skin flute. Billy's side-to-side sucking style, however, would be more suitable for the harmonica, his mouth swiftly gliding back and forth across the slick, shining strawberry shaft. It was beautiful music to his lecherous fan, but I had seen enough!

I told Billy I was going to the restroom and would return in about five minutes. I figured that would be ample time for him to finish dessert. I started to grab the keys when a customer approached the counter with a few magazines. Perfect timing! This would allow me to concentrate on training Billy, who would need both hands free— meaning, thankfully, he would have to part ways with his beloved sucker.

I was the real sucker for thinking this!

The customer was a regular, and regulars know when foreigners are on their turf. "Training another one, Dré?"

"Yep."

Billy addressed the customer, holding the sucker in his right hand. "Is that all, boss?"

"That'll do it!"

I ripped a sheet off the paper-towel roll to give to Billy, the idea being that he would use it as a wrap for his candy while helping the customer. That wouldn't be necessary, however, as Billy took advantage of the situation to truly show off his oral skills, deep-throating the entire piece of candy! All that remained was an inch of white stick protruding from his glossy puckered lips—along with a spittle of drool running down his chin. Somewhere, Linda Lovelace was smiling ... along with Billy's fan!

I didn't feel so badly now, because the witness standing at the counter was likewise astonished by the accident across the lane. He gazed at me to make sure I was seeing what he was seeing ... to make sure he wasn't dreaming! He needed a pinch!

What I offered instead was a don't-worry-it-will-all-be-over-soon nod of the head and smile.

The transaction took less than two minutes, although the experience seemed to last for two hours. One thing is for sure: Once the transaction was finished, it took my regular less than *two seconds* to flee the scene! "Good luck with that one, Dré!"

Confused, Billy repeated, "Good luck with *that one*? Did I do something wrong?"

Outside of violating about ten different guy codes? Nah! I couldn't say aloud what I was thinking, so instead, I told Billy, "That guy has been coming here for a long time, and he's seen a lot of people come and go. It's his way of saying hopefully, you'll be sticking around."

"Oh, because for a second, I thought maybe he had a problem with me eating this sucker?"

"Really?"

"Yeah."

"What makes you say that?"

"A feeling—you know like when something just doesn't feel right?"

"I'm familiar."

Billy had finally finished his treat, tossing the stem and wrapper in the trash. "That was actually pretty good! I suppose it might seem a bit strange to see another guy eating one of those."

Billy, it does have the makings of a potentially awkward situation."

"Well, André, I thank you for not making me feel uncomfortable.

Some people can be really immature at times." "I know, right?! Don't you just hate that?"

"Yeah."

"Me too, Billy."

THE CASE OF THE MISSING DIARY

From time to time, customers return rented movies in the wrong cases. The numbers written on the discs then don't correspond with the ones labeled on the cases, and because the cases are filed in numerical order, if a clerk doesn't make sure the numbers match when the DVDs are brought back, trying to sort them out later can be a tricky endeavor.

This is understandable, though. To be expected, really, a mathematical certainty due to the sheer number of rentals we do per day, some guys taking four or five movies at a time. Once at home, many hurry—for fear of being caught by a wife, girlfriend, or significant other—to watch the movies and in their haste put the DVD in the wrong case.

I'd say ninety-nine percent (a modest number) of customers couldn't care less if everything matches. They figure if they have returned all the DVDs on time and in good condition, that should be sufficient. They are right, this is what is most important; however, it would behoove all renters to exercise a bit of caution when returning movies they've watched at home. One would hate to bring in the wrong DVD, meaning that somewhere, there is quite possibly a movie where it *shouldn't* be—making a late fee the very *least* of their worries!

Enter a guy I had never seen before. He walked into the store carrying one of our signature black bags. The contents within caused a familiar bulge recognizable to my well-trained eye. I guessed he was returning movies.

"Hello, how are you this morning?" I greeted him.

"I am doing well, thanks," he replied. "I want to return these DVDs."

Yes, I am that good! Or perhaps I've been working this job for way too long. Probably the latter.

"How did you like them?" I inquired.

He disclosed that he had seen only bits and pieces of each movie because he only had an hour to watch them all, not to mention the constant interruptions. "My sixteen-year-old daughter kept coming downstairs every twenty minutes to get something out of the kitchen. Kinda kills the mood, you know?"

"I can imagine."

"Once, she even came into the living room where I was," he recalled. "She almost caught a glimpse of something I wouldn't want her to see. Luckily, I managed to switch channels in time. She grabbed some of her movies from underneath the television and went back upstairs."

"A narrow escape."

The empty box covers matching the discs rested on a shelf above my head. I reached up and brought them down before taking the DVDs out of the bag. There were three rentals. The first one was a match. The second one, a match. The third one, a problem—a big one!

I looked up at the customer. "So, um, does your daughter like Renée Zellweger?"

He looked at me, dumbfounded. "Why yes, how did you know?" he questioned.

"Well ..."

"Her and her friends like to have movie night on Fridays," he inserted. "As a matter of fact, the other night, I had to put away a bunch of DVDs they left scattered on the floor."

"Would one of those movies happen to have been *Bridget Jones's Diary*, by chance?"

"Dude, you are starting to freak me out!" His face was wrinkled with confusion. "How in the world did you know that?"

Slowly, I turned the disc around and watched his jaw appear to disjoint like one of those Burmese pythons on Animal Planet. His eyes bulged by the second. He even flinched suddenly, perhaps anticipating a slap to come later!

"Holy fuck!" he yelled. His face now distorted in distress. "I-AM-FUCKED!"

My first instinct was to look around the store to make sure no one had heard the outburst, like this crowd had never heard that type of language! My second was to try to calm the guy down, but that wasn't happening.

"I am *fucked*!" he screamed again.

"Try and relax for a sec—"

"Relax! Relax! You want me to *RELAX*?!"

"Yes, I want you to *relax*," I reiterated. "Just take *this* movie home and put it back in its original box—where, I'm sure, you will find our movie. No one will know."

"And I am sure that box, along with your movie, is on its way to a house full of young, unsuspecting teenage girls who are about to get the shock of their lives! *Everybody* will know!"

"What?!"

"My wife is taking my daughter over to a friend's house for a sleepover. They will be chatting on the phone, talking about boys, doing their nails, and eating junk food all while movies are playing in the background."

"Maybe that won't be one of the movies?"

"That's *always* one of the movies!"

Yep, you're fucked! I thought. Trying to think quickly to help the poor guy, I suggested, "Why don't you call your wife and tell her what's going on?"

He looked at me as if I'd just had the *worst* idea in the history of bad ideas. "She doesn't know I watch these movies! And if that isn't bad enough, imagine how she will react when she finds out my *daughter* has one—that's mine?"

"Imagine how a group of enraged mothers will react once they find out their daughters made the leap into sexual adulthood thanks to you?"

"I-AM-FUCKED!" he bellowed once more.

"Listen," I tried to convince him, "you have to call your wife and let her know. The alternative is much worse!"

"What if I can catch them before they watch the movie and do a quick exchange?"

"You mean like show up with the DVD and pretend you found it lying around the house and had to bring it to your daughter because you know her and her friends would be disappointed without it, then make the switch?"

On came the light bulb. "Yes! That's good. You're very good! It's only late afternoon, and they probably won't be watching movies until tonight. I just have to be slick about swapping the DVDs!"

"*Very* slick!" I emphasized. "You can't let her see the DVD label. Which movie was it, again?"

He lowered his head and mumbled, "*Poke That Tranny in the Fanny.*"

"Jesus."

"I need divine intervention at this point," he realized. "I'm not very religious, but if you are, call in a favor for me!" He juggled his car keys and told me hopefully, he would be back. If not, that meant my prayer had gone unanswered. For the sake of all those teenage girls, I hoped someone was watching out for the guy, even if he wasn't looking out for others, nearly knocking over a customer as he darted out the door.

"Hey, watch it!" the gentleman yelled.

"Sorry!" a voice screamed in the distance. "Are you all right?" I asked.

After brushing himself off and picking up his bag, the newcomer assured me, "I'm fine. That guy ran out of here like a bat out of hell! Where could he possibly be headed in such a hurry?"

"If he's not fast enough, *divorce!*"

"Huh?"

"Nothing, never mind." At that point, I felt it appropriate to offer an apology on behalf of the store. "Sorry about almost being tackled at the door! Generally, the welcoming committee greets customers in a much warmer fashion."

He chuckled. "It's all right, young man. He just caught me by surprise. There was a time in my life where that would never happen."

Really? Hmm. His comment got me thinking. What had he once been? A boxer? A football player? Martial artist? It was difficult to determine because now, well into his sixties, he had been deprived of all physical prowess by time.

I wouldn't have to wait long for the answer, however, as he provided it via his next question. "You look like fellow military. Are you?"

"No," I replied.

"Your buzz cut is what made me ask. That and you look angry like me!"

"Angry? I look angry? No, I'm not angry at all … wait, why are you angry?"

"A lot of veterans around my age are angry! You do your time and once you're done, the military says, 'Thanks for your service and good luck with the rest of your life!'"

"But the VA [Veterans Administration] has programs to help veterans assimilate to normal civilian life," I mentioned.

"Yes, but these programs didn't exist back when I served."

"When was that?"

"I fought in the Vietnam War and came out in 1978. It was a very psychological war. And a lot of the combat was up close and personal. Images that you never forget, memories that haunt you for the rest of your life."

I offered my sympathy. "I'm sorry to hear that."

"Yeah, me too! I was at a Stand Down recently in the Veterans Village of San Diego. Attending those events always help me out."

"What's a Stand Down?"

He proceeded to tell me that in wartime, a stand-down is a time when soldiers are removed from battle and taken to a place of relative safety and security, where they can rest and recover. The VVSD, organizers of the nation's first Stand Down in 1988, refers to a stand-down as a time when homeless veterans can remove themselves from the "combat of the streets" and allow the VVSD and the community of San Diego to "stand the watch" so they can receive needed services and rest.

"When I first got there," he recalled, "they served me coffee and breakfast. I went to this big tent and got to shower and shave." He unzipped his bag, reached inside, and pulled out a pamphlet. "Here, check this out!"

Indeed, this Stand Down was a veteran's utopia! It offered all the things he had mentioned—and more! A veteran's medical, dental, and optical issues are tended to, as well. Long-term needs are also addressed.

"The VVSD philosophy is 'a hand up, not a hand out,'" he said, "which I appreciate because we are a proud bunch."

Another benefit of the Stand Down is the sharing of experiences amongst veterans. "A vet who served in Afghanistan was telling me about the time he accidentally drove a truck over a land mine," he said. "The explosion blew up the truck, but they all survived."

"That's fortunate," I remarked.

"I told him he was very lucky, and then I told him why: 'Once in 'Nam, I saw a man walk over a land mine, and the explosion killed an entire squad. No survivors.'"

"Very unfortunate."

"Yes, it was. Witnessing casualties like that is why veterans of war never get over their problems. We have to learn to work through them."

"The problem I have found is that when veterans get back from war, they don't want to talk about what happened, which is counterproductive. Really, the only way to help manage the trauma is to talk about these suppressed feelings," I said.

My knowledge on the subject, albeit very limited, seemed to surprise him—enough for him to ask if I had ever been involved with any type of veteran-assistance programs.

"I have done work with the PAIRS foundation," I informed him. "What's PAIRS?"

It was now my turn to provide information. I pulled a card out of my wallet and read to him the PAIRS mission statement printed on the back:

> The mission of the nonprofit PAIRS Foundation, a 501(c)(3) charity, has been to teach those attitudes, emotional understandings, and behaviors that nurture and sustain healthy relationships and to make this knowledge broadly available on behalf of a safer, saner, more loving world. We accomplish our mission by developing and delivering evidence- based, best practices in marriage, family and fatherhood education, conducting research, and training instructors worldwide.

Once I finished, I mentioned that I not only had taken the PAIRS workshop but was also a certified first-level instructor. "I'm not surprised, because you seem to be a good communicator," he said to me. "You are very easy to talk to, and you make me feel very comfortable. I may have to look further into this program. The Stand Down I went to up north helped me the most in working through my main issues, but I still have some things unresolved."

"A PAIRS course would prove highly beneficial," I promised him.

He asked me for more information about the foundation, and I gave it to him, then thanked him for his service. And with that exchange, we parted ways. He went back to the booth area, and I went back to the newly donated leather chair behind the counter.

Sinking into its soft cushions, I tilted my head back and swiveled from side to side. I thought about how I had just talked to someone who had actually fought in the Vietnam War—and lived to tell about it! I also thought about someone who was off to fight a very different kind of war—one he might wish he wouldn't live to talk about. I *wouldn't* learn of his fate for weeks to come.

About a month later, I was doing a shift change with Greg. He told me a customer had come in and left a message for me.

"Who was it?" I asked.

"I'm not sure," Greg responded. "He didn't look familiar." "What did he say?"

"It was weird because I've never seen anyone so happy to return a movie! He said to tell you that he couldn't avoid the doghouse, but he did avoid the courtroom—whatever that means. What's he talking about?"

First, I grinned, which fast became a chuckle, which quickly turned into laughter. I then posed a question to Greg. "Do you believe in miracles?"

He gave me a strange look before replying, "Yes."

I smiled at him. "Well somebody just witnessed one."

CAUGHT IN THE MATRIX

I'd have to say of all the items in our store, enhancement pills garner the most attention. Customers want to know which ones work the best, which ones last the longest, which ones have side effects, and of course, which ones I have tried.

Any time I get grilled with any—or all—of these questions, I think about Morpheus. Yes, Morpheus. Yes, the one from the film *The Matrix*. He had it easy, having to worry about only *two* pills, the consumption of either leading to very different outcomes: one red, representing the choice to embrace the sometimes painful truth of reality, and one blue, representing the choice to remain in the blissful ignorance of illusion.

I, however, have pills that are red, blue, gold, silver, green, black, and white. And the fact that they are all marketed to achieve the *same* end, restoring sexual vitality, makes the customer's decision—and my job—even more difficult.

Further complicating matters are all the colorful names and suggestive imagery on the packaging. On one, a giant snake is pictured wrapped around the pill; on another, the pill is encased inside the picture of a giant rhinoceros's horn. A third has the pill inside a thermometer set to explode!

Even repeat customers who are experiencing great results with a specific pill still can't resist the urge to find something "even better": Fifteen minutes needs to be thirty minutes. Three days have to be six days. Two girls in one night at Motel 6 turns into an eight-person orgy in a Mexican villa.

Surprisingly, the average age of pill buyers gets younger by the year. I remember that when I first started in 2006, mostly older men looking for an alternative to Viagra would frequent the store for the pills. A decade later, it's not uncommon to find an eighteen-year-old purchasing a bottle of our most popular enhancement pills—and returning two weeks later to buy more, even though one pill is supposed to last up to five days and there are six pills in a bottle.

I wouldn't be surprised to learn that some of these customers have become so dependent upon the proprietary blends and other ingredients in these pills that they have a problem performing without them. Whether this is the case or not, their stories never cease to amaze me. Here are four of my favorites.

A middle-aged man in fairly good shape came up to the counter and stared intently at the products behind the glass. He marveled at our pill selection, his eyes widening as his brain attempted to process the influx of data. Uncertain of what to choose, he looked up at me, and the conversation began.

Customer: Hey, brother! What's the best thing you got?

André: This silver pill is the one I sell the most. Have you tried anything before?

Customer: Yeah, the gold one.

André: It didn't work?

Customer: Well, I bought one here and took it before I left.

André: And?

Customer: About five minutes later, I felt this "tingle." Before long, I was getting hard after every speed bump!

André: Question answered.

Customer: Oh yeah! I got this much younger girlfriend, and she told me I wore it out!

André: And you want better results than that? You shooting for paralysis?

Customer: Ha-ha! No, nothing like that. I was just wondering if you had something even stronger!

André: Well, generally, I tell customers if they find a pill that works well and doesn't cause any side effects, they should stick with that one. It's all about how well the ingredients mix with your body chemistry.

Customer: Right.

André: But if you are looking for something stronger that is safe as well, I would suggest the silver one. It is made by the same company but has 250 mg more proprietary blend than the gold one.

Customer: Oh, that's good … because I'm packing some heat!

Disturbingly enough, I wished he was referring to a gun.

André: Alrighty, then! That will be $12.95.

Customer: This girl is so hot! And we are exact opposites. I'm a thirty-eight-year-old bald white guy who used to be married. She is a twenty-four-year-old Mexican girl who has had only two boyfriends her entire life.

André: Opposites attract.

Customer: You are right! I'm 6'2", 220. She is 5'2", 110. I toss her around like a rag doll!

André: So you are trying to paralyze her.

Customer: Oh, she loves it! Here, let me show you a picture of her!

He flipped out his phone and began skimming through the images. He stopped at one and turned the face of the phone towards me. There she was, wearing a huge grin—nothing else!

He was right, though—she is hot!

Customer: Okay, let me show you this text message she left me.

André: Okay.

Customer: Check this out.

I took the phone again and looked at the screen. It had an emoticon of a winking smiley face, with the words next to it saying, "I'm okay. Just soar!" (Yes, that's how she spelled it.)

André: Wow.

Customer: I know, right?! Special, huh?

Special Ed, I thought.

Customer: And she hit on me first, can you believe that? I told her how old I was, and she asked me if I was going to show her some things!

Like how to spell?

André: You'd better be careful, or she may not let you go!

Customer: I hope she doesn't, because she is hot! Where am I going to find better at my age? I'll be back in a few weeks to update you.

André: Can't wait.

With that, he ran out the door, hopped into his fire-hydrant-red convertible, and sped off to dip into his fountain of youth.

What midlife crisis?

A teenager came barreling through the door. He didn't look a day over sixteen, so I checked his driver license. He'd been legal for a week.

Teenager: Man, I am so excited!

André: It will wear off after you have been in here a few hundred times, trust me.

Teenager: No, not that. I'm about to go fuck this stripper!

André: Oh, something I can relate to! That can be exciting. First time?

Teenager: Yeah! So you were with a stripper?

André: Mm-hm.

Teenager: How was it? Was she a freak? Was it like, the best sex you ever had?

André (laughing): Hmm. Let's see ... the sex was definitely memorable! Yes, she was a freak! And—

Teenager: I knew it! I can tell this girl would be the same way. Man, I've been after her for a few years and finally—

André: Whoa, wait a minute! A few years? You just turned eighteen, so how old is this girl?

Teenager: She is twenty, but she's been a stripper since she was eighteen.

André: Oh, okay.

Teenager: We've flirted over the last year or so, but she said she wouldn't take me seriously until I was *legal*!

André: That you are!

Teenager: Man, *fuck* voting! I think every guy should get to fuck a stripper once he turns eighteen!

André: Now there's a rite of passage!

Teenager: Any advice for me?

André: Well, you are definitely thinking smart, coming in to buy condoms.

Teenager: I already have condoms. I'm here to get a pill!

André: A pill! At your age?

Teenager: Yeah, man! I gotta get it in! I've been waiting a long time for this, and she said I better deliver since I've been talkin' all this shit!

André: Here's a bit of advice for future reference.

Teenager: What's that?

André: In instances like these, it is generally best to set the bar low. That way, you can only exceed expectation.

Now, the pressure is on! This may be your one and only shot— and you can't blow it!

Teenager: No pun intended, right?

André: Pun intended.

Teenager: See, now you've got me thinking—she probably has a few guys trying to fuck her, huh?

André: Is she hot?

Teenager: Yeah!

André: Quite a few!

Teenager: I knew it! I kinda figured that out last week when she took me to this bar.

André: For a birthday drink?

Teenager: Yeah. At one point, we went out on the dance floor, right? I swear, after about five minutes, it seemed like every guy there was watching her!

André: What did you expect? She's a stripper.

Teenager: How could they tell?

André: How could they not! Teenager: What do you mean?

André: Everything about a stripper—the way they walk, talk, and dance—oozes seduction. Their livelihood depends upon it. People around them pick up on that vibe, regardless of the location. A stripper can't just turn that off because there isn't a pole in front of her.

Teenager: Well, there sorta was a pole in front of her!

André: Pun intended, right?

Teenager: Right! Man, it's fun talking to you! What else can you tell me?

André: If your friend has been dancing for two years, chances are she's into women.

Teenager: Really?! You mean I could have a threesome with two strippers one day?

André: Possibly, depending upon how much she likes you.

Teenager: What do you mean?

André: Well, if she looks at you as someone to have fun with, then she won't mind bringing other girls into your relationship. But if she catches feelings, then she will be just like any other woman and will not want to share you.

Teenager: Damn, that would suck!

André: Well, it works both ways. Guys start out like you: happy to be sexing a stripper and cool with everything. Then at some point, they start to catch feelings and become jealous and possessive. Suddenly, they have a problem with "their girl" being half naked and rubbing up against other men.

Teenager: You know, I never thought of it that way.

André: Son, you're about to get pussy-whipped!

Teenager (laughing): Oh no! Not me. I *have* had sex before.

André: Not with a stripper.

Teenager: True. But I can't allow myself to catch feelings. And I'm not saying that because she is a stripper. … I'm saying that because I know she has a drug problem.

André: Meth, right?

Teenager: Yeah! Man, how do you know all this shit?

André: As someone once said to me, "Experience has taught me well!" A dancer's life can be all about long days and hard nights. Some of them need that pick-me-up to keep going.

Teenager: I believe it! One time she picked me up around two in the afternoon, and she was dead tired!

André: Busy night. She probably woke up thirty minutes before you saw her.

Teenager: What I remember most is stopping by this beauty supply store. She picked up a hairbrush and some hair dye. The total came to like $28. She gave the lady all ones!

André: (laughing): Tip money!

Teenager: Dude, I was so embarrassed!

André: You're going to be more than just embarrassed if you don't perform up to expectations.

Teenager: Aw, man! See, now you got me thinking about it again! What pill should I get?

André: Honestly, I don't think you need—

Teenager: Naw, man! Hook me up! I gotta fuck like a porn star tonight!

André: Oh, why didn't you say so? In that case, here is what you do. Got any uncles that you're close to?

Teenager: Yeah, as a matter of fact, I do! My uncle Tony.

André: How old is Uncle Tony?

Teenager: Uh, shit, probably late forties.

André: He still gettin' it in?

Teenager: For sure! Uncle Tony is a player!

André: Perfect! So, I want you to call up the stripper and postpone the date until tomorrow.

Teenager: *Tomorrow!* Why?

André: Because tonight, you are going to go see Uncle Tony and get some Viagra.

A short, stocky man came into the store. He was wearing a bright orange long-sleeved shirt decorated with splotches of dried concrete. His clean-shaven head glistened underneath a partially cracked construction helmet.

Customer: Say, man, do any of these pills *really* work?

André: Yes.

Customer: What's a good one?

André: The silver one is our best seller.

Customer: Really?

André: Yes.

Customer: Can I see the bottle?

André: Sure.

Customer: Actually, these do work. I'll take the bottle.

Wait a minute…

Customer: I get these all the time. I just wanted to see if you were up on your job!

André: *Right.*

Customer: Here's $60, that should do it!

Wait a minute...

Customer: Oh wait! You need more than that, don't you?

André: More testing, right?

Customer: Ha-ha. No. My bad. Hold on to that, and I'm gonna go get more out the ride.

André: Okay.

A few minutes passed before he reentered the store.

Customer: Here's the rest.

Transaction complete.

André: Here's your change.

Customer: You know, I used to work in a porn store.

André: Is that right?

Customer: Yeah. I would do payouts every day and *take* the money.

André: *Really* ... and you didn't get caught?

Customer: Naw. I probably would have, but I quit after about a year. Everybody was doing it, though. This one guy, Bob, was taking thousands!

André: They should have fired that bookkeeper and hired a knuckle breaker!

Customer: I know, right! Some *Casino* shit! The girl who was in charge was one dumb broad!

André: Blind and deaf, too?

Customer (laughing): All that! Do you know if you guys are hiring?

André: Not at this store, but we do have four others. You might wanna kick that habit of yours before applying, though.

Customer (laughing): The job isn't for me. It's for my girlfriend's son. The muthafucka is lazy beyond belief!

André: Sounds like he'd be a great addition to our team.

Customer: All he wants to do is lay on the couch, play video games, and smoke weed!

André: Ah ... the life.

Customer: Right?! At twenty-four! He went to Texas and played Arena League football for four months. Once it was over, he came home and went right back to Momma's couch!

André: Somebody needs to cut the cord.

Customer: Amen, brutha! I got him *two* job prospects! For one of them, all he had to do was go down to the shipyard and fill out the application. He brought the muthafucka back home!

André: He doesn't want a job.

Customer: He don't wanna work, do he?!

I nodded my head.

Customer: I told my girl to call the police and have him removed.

André: That's a bit drastic, isn't it? Can't you guys just tell him he's six years past his legal stay?

Customer: The muthafucka won't go! I told her to call the police and take his clothes to a friend's house. Wherever your clothes are— that's where you live!

André: *If* you get him out, are you guys ever going to let him come back?

Customer: Oh yeah! He can come back and visit all he wants. His ass just needed to be out, like, *yesterday*!

André: Well, good luck with that!

Customer: I'll tell you what you guys need ...

André: What's that?

Customer: A job pill! For lazy muthafuckas like this one!

Two older black men, approximately late fifties, came into the store. They walked over to the fetish wall and started inspecting the strap-ons with hollow dildo attachments. One complained about the prices. The other, who was holding a package, signaled for me.

Customer 1: Say, brutha man! Is this the largest size you have?

André: What size are you looking for?

Customer 1: I need a size 8 (inches). This is a size 6. This muthafucka too small!

Customer 2: That's what you say. The muthafucka probably too big!

Customer 1: Fuck you! You think you funny. The shit is too little!

André: Well, here's a size 8—but the attachment isn't black.

Customer 2 (laughing): Look at that shit! You gonna have a tan dick and you black as a muthafucka!

Customer 1: Nah, I can't fuck wit that one! She turn around and see that and the muthafucka will run straight out the door!

Customer 2: Man, just go ahead and get the size 6! It's cheaper anyway.

Customer 1: Why the muthafucka cheaper? Hey brutha, why the eight-inch cost more?

André: Because it's bigger.

Customer 2: You gotta pay for the shit you ain't blessed with!

Customer 1: Fuck you!

Customer 2: Will you just get the muthafucka and let's call it a day!

André: Oh wait! Here, I found a black one.

Customer 1: Good shit! I'll take that one. Brutha man, is your ATM working? I gotta pull out some more cash.

André: Yes, it is.

Customer 2: Don't forget, I owe you twenty dollars.

Customer 1: That's right! Never mind, brutha, I got enough cash. Let me buy this shit and get outta here.

We walked toward the counter.

André: Do you need anything else, or will that be all?

Customer 1: Naw, that's it. The bitch better be happy with that!

I rang up the sale and bagged the item.

André: Here is your receipt.

Customer 1: Naw! Throw that away, man! I can't have my wife finding that shit! And don't ball it up, either—rip up the muthafucka!

Customer 2: Say, man, do any of these pills *really* work?

André: Yes, they do.

Customer 1: I'll bet they don't! Have you ever tried one?

André: Yup.

Customer 1: And it worked?

André: Yup.

Customer 2: It's like *The Matrix* times twelve up in this muthafucka! How do you choose one pill? Red. Blue. Green. Silver. Shit!

André: The silver one is our best seller.

Customer 1: You ain't just sayin' that to get in a muthafucka's pockets, are you?

André: No, it *really* works! I can't guarantee you how well, though.

Customer 2: Man, you know you want the muthafuckin' pill. Just buy it!

Customer 1: I guess I could try the muthafucka out! All right, brutha man, lemme get that silver one. I got these two hoes comin' down from LA next week. I'm goin' Neo on them bitches!

Customer 2: Shit, if the muthafuckas work like that, give him a bottle! Then we won't have to come back and be all up in this muthafucka buying strap-ons and shit!

Customer 1: Fuck all that! If it don't work, I'm bringing them bitches back here to let brutha man deal with 'em!

After they left the store, I had easily come to my decision: Morpheus ... the blue pill, please!

SINCE MY LAST CONFESSION

The counter: the place to count change. The place to test toys. The place where many a future orgasm will have its beginning. For the store, it is quite simply the major thoroughfare through which all business is transacted. For me, it is the perfect ice-breaker. It is a microscope magnifying the thin line between morality and immorality. It is a gateway providing glimpses into a stranger's soul.

For some customers, it is a place to vent, openly and freely. It is a place to bond. It is a place of revelation. It is an instrument of catharsis. It is the ultimate confessional. I do not condone the practice of confessing one's transgressions to a person who isn't the victim of said wrongdoing for forgiveness; I do, however, firmly believe that verbalizing one's thoughts and feelings instead of internalizing them is essential to a person's mental well-being.

Sometimes people just want to talk. They want to unload emotional baggage they have carried around for far too long. They want to lay their burdens down—at the counter!

I had not seen Tyree in a while. He was what we called a part-timer. The part of the time he was long absent from the store, we knew that probably meant he was "doing a bid."

Tyree was always very warm and cordial to the clerks, but we all suspected he dabbled in illegal activities. He had a tattoo on his neck signifying his gang affiliation, in addition to markings on his arms and back, but he was never disrespectful or confrontational. In fact, I never had a problem with him. None of us did.

The other customers in the store knew him, too, and not one of them ever voiced a complaint about him, which is rare for a place that can be one step above high school in terms of petty antics and silly gossip.

One day, Tyree greeted me as he always did upon entering the store, but I could sense there was something troubling him. He paced back and forth in front of the counter.

"Everything all right, Tyree?"

"Man, I got to get out of Lemon Grove! It's been nothing but trouble for me ever since I came here." He walked over to the water fountain. He took his hands out of his hooded sweatshirt long enough to pour himself a cup of water. "The police came and raided the house I'm living at last night," he said. "I got this feeling something was going down, and I told my girl I needed to get out of there. So, I left her on the couch."

"She didn't want to go with you?"

"No, she thought I was just being paranoid. As I was walking to the store, I saw five or six cop cars racing down the street. I *knew* where they were going, so I went to a friend's house. I called my girl this morning, and sure enough, she said the cops had taken two of our roommates to jail."

"Good intuition."

"I tell these youngsters there are no more hustles left out there, you will get caught, but they are at that age when they think they know everything and are smarter than everyone else. I used to be that way when I was deep in the drug game."

This was new information, but not at all surprising. Tyree looked and carried himself like someone who was wise in the ways of street life. What I didn't expect was for him to start opening up to me now, just minutes after seeing me for the first time in almost a year. We'd never really talked before about his personal life, but for some reason, he felt now was the time to do so.

"You know, it's very easy to talk to you," Tyree said. "I usually keep to myself about things, but you make me feel very comfortable."

(This wouldn't be the last time that day that I would be paid this compliment.)

I thanked him and attributed it to all the years of listening to the stories of people I had interviewed as a journalist, as well as to customers who regaled me daily with their tales of astonishment as Tyree was doing presently.

"When I was young, I grew up right next to the border," Tyree continued. "All my homies were Mexican." (Tyree is black.) "We used to 'pull licks' all the time, going back and forth to Tijuana. I remember once, we did a deal a day before my birthday, and I blew all the money at a club celebrating with the homies!"

Tyree informed me that everyone in his group had different jobs. His was to help oversee the operation to ensure everything went smoothly. One of his best friends had been in charge of storing and distributing their product. "In his house, there was a back wall that opened and was stacked with (drugs) from the floor to the ceiling," Tyree revealed. "He also did real estate, so he would use some of the vacant properties as stash houses. If he got a tip they were going to raid his house, he would move the stuff to one of those spots. He would also send us to the houses to pick up the packages when we made deals."

Unfortunately for Tyree's entourage, their fate would prove true the adage; "live fast, die young." "The lifestyle took all my homies, though," Tyree mumbled before taking a final sip of water and tossing his cup in the trash. "The deal was supposed to be a simple pick up and drop ... but it turned into a disaster!"

Apparently, Tyree was supposed to meet his friends in Tijuana once he got off work from his regular job in construction. He said he was anxious all day. "I *felt* something. That night when I got home, I showered, ate, and took a nap. They were already there and were supposed to call me. But they never did!"

The next morning, Tyree got a phone call—but not the one he was expecting. "The homey called me and told me to turn on the news. They showed a crime scene down in Tijuana. My homies got 'caught up' and were made examples of by the Mafia in Mexico. The pictures of their dismembered bodies were on the cover of *La Alarma*, the Mexican newspaper. It shook me up! *Bad!* Still does, actually. That could have been ... should have been ... me too!"

More than twenty-five years have passed since that episode in Tyree's life. He hasn't been back to Mexico since. "I'll probably never go back. Too many memories. Not all bad, but that image of my homies still haunts me to this day."

Sentimental reasons aren't the only ones that keep Tyree on this side of the border. There is also the matter of his safety. "The drug game is tightly connected," he went on. "Someone knows someone who knows someone who knows you! That's why people get out the game and still get 'touched' years later. Someone recognized them for something they did long ago. There are no statutes of limitations in unlawful activities."

We were briefly interrupted by the distinctive sound of clinging bells, which signified movement at the door. In strutted a thick, curvy redhead. She passed by Tyree, batted an eyelash at me, and continued to the fetish wall.

I recognized that wink! There was something vaguely familiar, yet completely foreign, about this female.

Tyree sensed my internal struggle to identify her. Or perhaps my gawking made him uncomfortable. "You know her?" he whispered while leaning against the counter.

"Uh, I *think* so ... but I'm not sure," I mumbled back. "I see so many people. She could just remind me of someone else. It's not important. You were saying?"

When Tyree picked up his story, he admitted that he was no stranger to prison, where he was always put in a precarious position, being black but belonging to a Mexican gang. "It was tough at first because the brothers wanted to test me and some of the Mexicans had a problem with my color. But the esés had my back. Eventually, they all accepted me once I put in work."

Tyree's job was to keep peace between the two rival gangs. "The brothers knew that I understood their problems, being a black man. And I could communicate and relate to the Mexicans because I spoke fluent Spanish and grew up around them for most of my life. I was in prison six months, and they didn't have any problems. The day I got out, a riot broke out."

Tyree walked back over to the water cooler for more refreshment. He took a few long sips, then continued his retrospection. "My grandma didn't raise me like this," he acknowledged. "She was a God- fearing Christian woman from Texas!"

"So what happened?"

"I just got caught up running with the homies! I wasn't always into gangs. I used to do other things."

"Like what?"

"I used to be into break dancing!"

"Really?"

"Yeah! Once, I went on this audition with my boy to be in a commercial for Alpha Beta, but we used his phone number as the contact number and when we got a callback, he never told me."

"That's fucked up!"

"It is, but he didn't get the spot either."

"Karma."

"Yup! And when breakin' played out, I got into bikes."

"Motorbikes or bicycles?"

"Bicycles! Doing tricks. I was good, too! I was going to be a sponsor for BMX, but that is around the time I started to get heavy into the gang life."

Fortunately, the sins of the father weren't passed down to the son. "I have a boy, and he reminds me of myself before I got involved with gangs," Tyree said with a warm smile. "He is the one good thing in my life."

"How old is he?"

"Nineteen. I am so proud of him." Tyree balled up his second empty cup and dumped it in the trash. "He's quiet, polite, and very respectful. He's going into the Navy. It brings tears to my eyes, man."

"As far as manners go," I told him, "he sounds a lot like his dad."

"Thanks, André. I tell him not to be like me and make the same mistakes I did."

"What did he say to that?"

"He looked at me and said, 'Dad, don't worry. I'm not going to be anything like you!'"

We laughed.

"Man, André, I feel so much *lighter*! I hadn't talked to anyone about these things in a long time—if ever. Thanks for listening."

"Any time. If you ever need an ear, I have two!"

"Thanks again! You have a good day, man."

Tyree circled around the A-frames and made his way to the booth area. A few minutes later, the redhead approached the counter and revealed her true identity. "So, can a woman bend one of those ears, or is that a privilege reserved only for *men*?" her voice sharply inquired.

"Excuse me?"

"You know, what you just told that guy about being here for him if he needed an ear?"

"Oh that!"

"Yes, that!"

"Well, I have known him for a while and he just started unloading, so … who am I to stop a person from a much-needed vent?"

"So you wouldn't stop me?"

"Uh, well, I haven't stopped anyone in eight years, so why start now? I guess you could say I'm an equal-opportunity sounding board."

"Good answer. Besides, you know me anyway."

"I do?"

She made a slow deliberate turn toward me, walked up to the counter, and began tapping on the glass. Her piercing green eyes cut through my resolve. "Yes, we know each other … and I still do not see the heretic's forks or Spanish ticklers you promised me!"

"Oh! The dominatrix!"

She had dyed her hair since the last time I had seen her, which was why I'd had trouble recognizing her.

"Yes. And it's not good to lie to me!"

"Well … I was joking when … I mean, I was semi-serious when I … uh, did you happen to see the new stuff I put up?"

"Yes, and I'm still not impressed! But you are still rather entertaining."

"Well, at least there is that!"

"I came back here looking for a pump that swells up the clit."

"A pussy pump!"

"Yes! If my clit is really swollen, then I can put a vibrator to it and orgasm. That's really the only way I can have one."

"I'm sorry," I apologized regretfully, "we had two in stock, but we are currently sold out."

"Do you guys have any hypoallergenic lube, then? The regular lubes make me break out."

"Yes, we do have that!" I directed her to the lube display. "It's on the second shelf, right above the edible underwear."

"I've been with my boyfriend for nine years. And when you're with a man—especially a black man—for that long, you have to be willing to try different things to keep him. You know what I'm talking about!"

It's a black thang! Some of you will understand.

"Well, after nearly a decade, whatever you are doing must be working!"

"I thought so, too, until I found out he had a little something on the side," she grumbled. "You know how y'all can be!"

It's a man thang! All of you will understand.

Surprisingly, the fact that her significant other had cheated wasn't the worst part of the offense. "What angered me the most was the fact that he didn't tell me," she divulged. "Listen, if people who were married twenty-plus years broke up after a lapse in judgment, they would never make it to the twenty-year mark."

True. Unfortunately, however, she did not apply such logic when it came to her response to said indiscretion. "I found out he was at his dad's house, and I broke out the window!" she said, laughing as she looked back at her behavior. "I was on the phone with my sister, and she kept telling me not to do it, but the more she kept saying it, the more I wanted to throw that brick!"

Apparently, out-of-control behavior cannot be assigned to a specific gender—or race. "You hear people say don't make a black woman angry ... but you don't want to *piss off* a crazy white girl, either!"

Lines like this one are what make the dominatrix one of my more memorable customers. Of course, it pales in comparison to her signature statement, uttered some six months prior. "You know," I remind her, "you once said something that myself and everybody I have told still laugh about to this day."

She was too busy reading the labels on the back of the lube bottles to look up at me, but she still managed to ask, "Which was?"

"I asked you before what made you choose your current profession, and you answered, 'I hate men!'"

"I do hate men!" she promptly declared. "I was molested *three* times."

"Oh ... I see."

"The first time, I was only seven. That's how I lost my virginity— of course. When I was a teenager, my self-esteem was pretty low and I started prostituting for a while. As a matter of fact, I *still* do tricks on the side."

Stop the presses! It was wrong for her boyfriend to sleep with another woman, but it was all right for her—at her discretion—to sleep with other men? Just a tad hypocritical, no? You know what, it doesn't matter. I'm not going there after what she just revealed to me. I'm gonna leave it alone. I don't want to ask an inappropriate question, come off as being insensitive, seem in- considerate.

"So how does *that* work, exactly?!" (Men can be jerks.)

"What's *that*, exactly?"

Tread lightly, I reminded myself. "You can fuck other people, but your boyfriend can't?" (Real jerks.)

"There's a big difference in *that*!" "'Pray tell, what might *that* be?"

"The difference is," she explained, "I don't hide what I do from him. He knows what's going on. But he had this little fling and didn't tell me. I'm real about what I do, and he needs to be, too!"

"Okay. I can respect that."

"*Gee*, I'm glad. Probably wouldn't have been able to sleep if you didn't."

"*Sleep* ... where do you find the time in between your scheduled beatings and other extracurricular activities?"

Her stoic expression made the situation momentarily hard to read. If I had to venture a guess, I would say her intentions lay somewhere between laughing at me and lunging for my throat. Thankfully, the dominatrix had a sense of humor.

"No need to concern yourself with such details," she said. "Just know in all my dealings, I say who, I say—"

"When!"

We looked at each other and simultaneously blurted out, "*Pretty Woman!*"

It was then time for *my* confession. "You know, as chick flicks go, I liked that one."

"That movie was *completely* unrealistic and total bullshit!"

So much for a bonding share.

"Where the hell is my Edward Lewis?!" she griped.

"You probably scared him off with a *cock-and-ball* tie!"

"If that's the case, then he wasn't the right man for me!"

Resurfacing, Tyree glanced at the dominatrix as he headed toward the door. The two briefly made eye contact, then he nodded at me and left.

Turning back to me, the dominatrix admitted, "It's surprising how comfortable I am around you. You're very easy to talk to." (See, there it was again.) "You don't make me feel like I'm being judged, and you don't try to explain my behavior."

"You mean I don't say things like, 'You dominate men and select those you sleep with because it allows you to feel the control you didn't have when you were younger.' Shit like that?"

"Yeah. Shit *just* like that!"

"Well, one thing I have learned from our brief conversations is that you are very much aware of your situation. ... Your reactions could use a little work, though."

"Hey! A slight lapse in judgment and a girl is marked for life?"

"Well, you are the expert at leaving marks."

She giggled—a first—then realized she was running late for an appointment.

A bit intrusively, I asked, "What kind of appointment? Will the question be 'May I help you' or 'May I hurt you?'"

She laughed. "The first one! I don't have anything fun scheduled for today, although I thoroughly enjoyed our conversation."

Smiling back at her, I replied, "Likewise."

"I look forward to seeing you again," she told me, waving goodbye.

Unfortunately, that would never happen. I didn't see Tyree for quite a while after that either, but I knew what that meant! As for the dominatrix, I hoped she hadn't suffered a similar fate—I don't think she takes well to being the one confined.

A few weeks later, I got a visit from Davis. I hadn't seen him in close to two years. He was holding up well. A very bad experience with a near-fatal attraction had put him through the emotional ringer. It had gotten so bad that he had dropped an unhealthy amount of weight and fallen into a deep depression.

On this day, he burst through the door with his trademark ear-to-ear grin and vigorously shook my hand. "Man, it is *so* great to see you!" he exclaimed.

"Likewise, my friend," I replied. "How have you been?"

"Blessed, blessed! First off, let me ask, how is your mother?"

"She's good!"

Davis was from the South—Louisiana, in fact, which is my mom's home state. He was very much the Southern gentleman and was a momma's boy, much like myself. Our conversations often centered around our families, sports, and his one-time albatross named Amanda (the near-fatal attraction).

"There are two things that I can't believe," Davis said. "How I could ever allow myself to get involved with that girl ... and why I stayed in that mess with her for so long?" These questions were rhetorical, of course, as both Davis and I already knew the answers. This was simply an admission of his own stupidity in light of the blinding clarity provided by years of hindsight. (Been there, done that.)

———•••—●—•••———

Amanda was a gold digger in every since of the word. She had expected Davis to financially support her shopping whims in addition to helping her pay bills. She had thrown violent tantrums in his car that included slapping him across the face—while he was driving— and spitting on his dashboard. And it hadn't been uncommon for her to discuss their sex life with other women at their church— particularly when he underperformed in her estimation. (She's still out there, guys!)

"Even though I stood erect, emotionally and psychologically, I was on my knees!" Davis professed. "It was like I was being weighed down by demonic forces."

"I don't think Lucifer wanted to take her off your hands!" We both laughed and gave each other dap, knocking our fists together as a form of respect.

"André, every time I drive by the store, I think about our talks and how much you've helped me. I remember way back in 2012, coming up to this counter and proceeding to talk to you about my problems. Time after time, you were there for me."

"There's been enormous growth on both of our parts, Davis. I have learned as much from you as you have from me."

"Really?"

"Definitely! You—and others like you—have taught me how to truly listen instead of just waiting until a person is finished talking in order to provide whatever answer I thought they needed to hear. Not to mention listening without anxiousness, expectation, or judgment."

"Well, sir, you are very welcome. And André, you are very much appreciated!"

"The feeling is mutual, Davis."

"You don't know how much it meant to me to be able to come in here and cry out to someone who just listened and supported me. Thanks again!"

"You're welcome, Davis!"

(You're all welcome!)

HALL OF FAME/WALL OF SHAME

A clipboard full of papers hangs on a wall beside the counter. Splattered across these pages are photographs of the store's known violators, miscreants, and other garden-variety troublemakers. They have all earned a coveted spot on the infamous "Wall of Shame."

They run the gamut of undesirables: bothersome tweakers, counterfeit-bill passers, conspiring couples, lube bandits, hookers in training, wannabe pimps. Even one cross-dressing lingerie thief. "Oh my God!" a trainee once shrieked after seeing his picture. "Look at this guy! The police have him in handcuffs, walking him out the door

… and he is wearing a lace corset with fishnet stockings."

The best was yet to come, though. "Hold on a second …" She paused. "Is that …?"

Wait for it. "Oh my God!" Bingo!

"His *schlong* is sticking out!"

"Why yes, it is, in all its three-inch glory," I verified, having seen the snapshot more times than I care to say—once being too many!

Whenever someone new is hired to work at the store, we make it a point to familiarize them with the "Eighty-Sixed List." Members of this banned bunch (yes, we have many colorful names to describe them) tend to resurface weeks, months, sometimes years later in hopes of gaining access back into the establishment.

Unfortunately for them, along with the dubious distinction of making it on the wall comes a lifetime—or sufficient time so everyone who knows them has found other employment—ban. "Man, you guys are serious," the trainee remarked when I explained all of this to her. "These photographs are hysterical, though! I could sit here all day and look through them."

"That's good! Familiarize yourself with those pictures, because if you work here, you will need to recognize those faces."

"You even have comments under the captions," she noticed. "'Passes bad bills.' 'Fake credit card guy.' 'Bonnie-and-Clyde Fleshlight bandits.' 'Mr. Pee-body' ... *Mr. Pee-body?*"

"Yes. Mr. Pee-body." "What did he do?"

"He liked to 'make it rain' in the booths without spending any money."

"Huh?"

Wait for it.

"Oh my God!"

Bingo!

"Ew! Ew! Ew! That's gross!"

"Yes, it is," I agreed, "in addition to being disrespectful, unsanitary, and downright *disgusting*!"

Despite the slight trauma, it's always fun for employees to unveil pictures like these to innocent eyes. The shock value is immeasurable, the entertainment value priceless. "I love getting those types of responses from the trainees," Mark, one of the store clerks, said while I was retelling the story. "I get a kick out of watching them squirm—especially the girls!"

Mark had invited me, Chris, and Junior to his house one Saturday night for one of our male-bonding sessions. Junior was the only one among us who didn't work at the store, but being one of Mark's closest friends, he was often invited to hang out with us.

Chris had orchestrated this gathering to broach other subjects: specifically, basketball, football, and boxing. After reading the story about Ice-T, Chris was eager to see more of my publications, and once he'd told Mark and Junior that sports was my area of expertise, they had insisted I come over with articles in hand, so I had spent the previous night searching for six or seven stories that could possibly satisfy their sports cravings.

Rubbing his hands together, Chris asked me, "Did you bring your articles?"

"Yeah, I got 'em."

"All right, then, break 'em out! Let's get down to business!"

I laid my first article out on the living room coffee table. It was dated June 5, 1994. Mark quickly snatched it up, and our discussion began.

Mark: Wait, here is a *baseball* story. No fucking way! You interviewed Darryl Strawberry?

André: No, I didn't. The *City Times* wanted to do a story on him because he went to one of the local high schools that we covered. My boss researched that story, and I wrote the article.

Mark: Still, dude. That's awesome! I loved Strawberry when he was on the New York Mets!

André: He was a Los Angeles Dodger at that time.

Junior: Read the story, Mark.

Mark: It's four pages long! Here, I'll go over the highlights.

He began.

> "The sweet-swinging savior.
>
> That's the way that Darryl Strawberry was heralded upon his return to Los Angeles in 1991. Strawberry's unique blend of speed and power was supposed to make him L.A.'s new miracle worker when he was signed as a free agent by the Dodgers. Perhaps those weight-of-the-world expectations are the reason he failed ... Three years of Strawberry's life, marred with back ailments, fans' jeers and a bout with substance abuse, was finally over.

Few felt the pain and anguish that the prodigal son experienced more than those at his alma mater, Crenshaw High School. "It's pretty sad what happened to his career in Los Angeles because he had such high hopes," said Brooks Hurst, who coached Strawberry, who graduated in 1980, when he was a Cougar.

"When Darryl came back, he was really excited about playing in Los Angeles and seeing his former friends," former Crenshaw baseball star and major-leaguer Chris Brown said. "But the (bad) element has been around and worked against him." Brown, who played for the San Francisco Giants, San Diego Padres and Detroit Tigers, worked out Strawberry and former Dodger Eric Davis at Rancho Park last winter.

The three were friends as teenagers while playing for Earl Brown Jr. on a youth team called the Compton Moose ... Chris Brown was impressed with Strawberry's work ethic and expected his friend "to have a super season in 1994."

But that scenario did not play itself out, largely because of Strawberry's fishbowl existence and those who swam in his circle. "Strawberry's friends are from another world," said Earl Brown Jr. "They got as much money as he has but they got it the wrong way. He can't seem to shake them loose. He has to let them live their lives and he has to live his."

Troubled by his poor play, Strawberry's off-the-field problems began to escalate, friends said. While on the disabled list, he missed a rehab session on June 25, 1993.

Three months later, he was arrested for allegedly striking Charisse Simon, his live-in girlfriend. Simon did not file charges and the two were married Dec. 3.

During the October brush fires, Strawberry said during a radio interview: 'Let it burn. I don't live there anymore.'

On March 3, the IRS and U.S. attorney's office began to investigate Strawberry's alleged failure to file tax returns on more than $300,000 of income derived from autograph and memorabilia shows.

(Hurst) blames the Dodgers for not acting properly to treat (Strawberry's) injury. "Doctors have been throwing dice with Strawberry's career and I think that led to his depression and substance abuse," Hurst said.

Chris Brown said Strawberry did not consult his friends about his problems. "He likes to keep things to himself. I told him I would always be there whether he made 20 cents or $20 million," he said.

"I wish him the best of luck," said Crenshaw baseball coach Major Dennis. "I hope he comes back and plays somewhere. He is the best ball- player I know."

Junior: He came back and got those rings with the New York Yankees in 1996 and 1998.

André: And another in '99!

Junior: Yeah, that's right!

Mark: I didn't know he went to Crenshaw. I see you mentioned Eric Davis. Where did he go to high school?

André: Fremont.

Mark: Did you guys cover them, too? André: Yes, sir.

Mark: Damn! How many schools did you guys cover?

I couldn't remember them all off the top of my head, so I pulled out another paper from my stash to aid my memory. It was a February 21, 1993, issue that featured the Los Angeles City 4-A and 3-A Boys' Basketball Playoff Preview, complete with rosters.

André: All right, let's see here: Crenshaw, of course. Loyola, Dorsey, Fremont, Locke, Los Angeles, Manual Arts, South Gate, Huntington Park, Washington, Bell, Bell Gardens, Belmont, Birmingham, Franklin, Garfield, Roosevelt, Jefferson, Lincoln, Wilson, Jordan, Marshall.

Junior (sarcastically): That's it, huh?

André: All I can see. There may be a few other schools not listed here that I can't recall.

Junior: Did you have a favorite school to cover?

André: The Shaw!

Mark: Crenshaw?

André Yup.

Junior: Why? What was so special about them?

André: You've obviously never lived in Los Angeles. Where do I start? Well, the Crenshaw boys' basketball team was the bread and butter of the City Times Sports section the three years I was there. They won back-to-back city and state titles in 1993 and '94. I did a story on their coach, Willie West, who was a legend in high-school coaching circles. As a matter of fact, I brought the article. It was my first major story for the paper. It turned out to be one of my best works, not to mention one of my favorites.

Junior: Were you nervous?

André: No ... I was terrified! Coach West was a very private man and didn't like to open up to outsiders—particularly members of the press. Negative articles had been written about him and his program in the past, so to say he was skeptical of me would be an understatement.

Chris: I'll take *that* one, now that we're off fuckin' baseball!

Mark: What do you have against baseball?

Chris: Other than the fact that it's fuckin' boring? Nothing at all.

André: I'll admit, it took a minute to get used to covering baseball. But once I did, it was actually relaxing and enjoyable.

Chris: Yeah, yeah, whatever! So, Kris Johnson, son of Marques Johnson, played for Crenshaw and averaged twenty-two points and eleven rebounds?

Mark: Wait a minute, *the* Marques Johnson?! The one who played for the Milwaukee Bucks alongside Sidney Moncrief and Paul Pressey?

André: One and the same. Marques also played for John Wooden at UCLA, which is eventually where Kris decided to go. Chris, read the names of some of the other former players—although I know you don't know any of them.

Chris: Shit, I wasn't even born yet! It says here: "In 1983, John Williams led Crenshaw to its first State Championship as an at-large entry. Williams led Crenshaw to its seventh City championship the following year, and also won his second consecutive City Player of the Year award. He averaged 26 points during the regular season, 30 during the playoffs. Williams played two seasons at Louisiana State University, then made himself available for the NBA draft. He played four seasons with the Washington Bullets before he was acquired by the Clippers."

Mark: Wait, that's Hot Plate! Chris: Who?

André (laughing): Yeah, that's what they used to call him.

Chris: Why? What kind of a fuckin' nickname is Hot Plate?

André: Unfortunately, the kind given to a good player who battled with weight issues for most of his career. Many people I used to talk to believed Williams could have been a hall-of-fame player if he could have kept his weight under control. Chris, tell them about Stevie Thompson.

Chris: "In 1984-85, Crenshaw defeated Logan High School (Union City), 72-62, in overtime to win its second State title and finish the season 31-0. The Cougars were led by City Player of the Year Stephen Thompson, who also helped Crenshaw win the 1986 State championship, the school's third in four years."

André: The same Stevie Thompson who balled with my boys Derrick Coleman, Sherman Douglas, and Rony Seikaly on the 1986-'87 Syracuse University national runner-up team.

Mark: I hated that team! I'm glad Indiana University beat them on that last-second shot by Keith Smart!

André: Moving along.

Mark: So what did Marques do at Crenshaw?

André: Chris, educate the man.

Chris (handing the paper to Mark): Here, *you* read it!

Mark (flipping through pages): Uh, oh ... okay. I found it. "From 1971-73, under Mar-ques Johnson's leadership, Crenshaw did not lose. During the 1971-72 season—with a starting five of Renard Murray, Maynard Brown, Reggie Mims, Kenny Daniels and Mar-ques Johnson—Crenshaw averaged 70 points and surrendered only 45 a game. The Cougars had a 14-0 record with two games left in the season, but they were disqualified from playoff consideration for having an ... *ineligible player?*"

Junior: Busted! That sucks to have an undefeated season end like that.

André: All it did was piss Crenshaw off! Keep reading, Mark.

Mark: "One year later, Marques Johnson led an 18-0 Crenshaw team to its second City title in three years with a 79-74 victory over Jordan in the championship game. Marques Johnson was named City Player of the Year after averaging 26 points a game and 'as many rebounds as he wanted,' Willie West said."

Junior: Damn! I never knew Crenshaw had players like that!

Mark: Listen to this: "Crenshaw averaged 23 wins a season and never lost more than five games in a season with West as coach. During a six-year span, between 1983-89, they won five City titles and made the City playoff semifinals 20 consecutive years."

Junior: Boy, I bet you were spoiled covering that program?

André: You have no idea.

Mark: Marques and Hot Plate gave West props, too! Marques put him up there with Wooden and Don Nelson as far as coaching goes. Hot Plate said he is "in the same class as Morgan Wooten [DeMatha High School, Washington D.C.], Mike McLeese [Dunbar High School, Washington D.C.] and Bob Hurley Sr. [Jersey City, N.J.]."

Junior: That's Bobby Hurley's dad, right?

Mark: Yes.

Chris: Ya got anything on some current players, perhaps someone who has played since I've been born?

Junior: Aw, somebody is feeling left out.

André: Not to worry, Chris. Think of this as a G-rated presentation: It's suitable for all ages.

Mark and Junior found humor in my comment, Chris, not so much, so I handed him a copy dated July 3, 1994.

André: Look at the Sports section.

Chris (turning to the back): See, *this* is what I'm talkin' 'bout! Junior: What ya got?

Chris: It's talking about the high-school summer camps and tournaments ... but I'm looking at the names. *Jesus!* Kevin Garnett. Stephon Marbury. Vincent Carter. Ron Mercer. Paul Pierce.

Mark: Oh shit!

Junior: Damn, Dré! You were on it like that?!

André: Mm-hm.

Mark: What's it say about Garnett?

Chris: "The Nike All-American All-Star Camp (Deerfield, Ill.) will showcase many of the nation's best high school seniors including top prospect, Kevin Garnett, a 6-foot-10 center from Mauldin (S.C.) High School. 'Garnett is the most gifted all-around big man I've seen in 20 years,' said Bob Gibbons, publisher for *Lenoir*, N.C.-based All Star Sports Publications. 'He is an amazing shot-blocker, has an excellent feel for the game and does instinctive things on the court that can't be taught.'"

Junior: First-ballot NBA Hall of Famer!

Mark: No doubt. What's it say about Starbury?

Chris: Umm ... "Stephon Marbury, a [6'3"] point guard from Brooklyn (N.Y.) Lincoln High, will headline the list of talent at the Adidas ABCD at Teaneck, N.J. 'Marbury is better than Kenny Anderson was at that stage,' said Clark Francis, editor and publisher of the *Hoop Scoop magazine*."

A Feast for Basketball Gourmets

Summer Camps Offer a Look at Some of the Country's Most Talented Young Players

By CHARLES SMITH / SPECIAL TO THE TIMES

André: Pierce and Shareef Abdur-Raheem were at that camp, too. You guys remember Reef?

Mark: Yup.

Junior: Me too.

Chris: So, did you actually see any of them play? André: Pierce.

Mark: Wow!

André: Yeah, I saw him play against André Miller.

Junior: Seriously?

André: Yeah! Inglewood High (Pierce's high school) and Verbum Dei (André's high school) played in a preseason game—one of the best high-school basketball games I've ever seen.

Mark: Who won?

André: Inglewood won in overtime by a few points. From what I can remember, Pierce had about thirty-seven points and André had, like, thirty.

Mark: Two future hall of famers going at it!

André: I don't know if André will get in, but I'm proud of what he's done at his size.

Junior: Yeah. He is only, what, about 6'2"?

André: Somewhere around there. He was a shooting guard in high school, but his college coach, Rick Majerus (Utah), converted him to point guard, and that's what has allowed him to have a long-lasting career. He's a hall-of-fame person, though. Great guy!

Mark: He seems like it. You never hear about him getting into any type of trouble or altercations like a lot of other athletes. And he just goes about his business on the court, never saying anything.

André: I have a story I wrote about trash talking in basketball, and the one quote I got from André speaks to what you just said.

I opened the paper from January 30, 1994.

André: "Verbum Dei leading scorer André Miller, who averages 24 points, is one of the few area players who posts big numbers without the fuss. 'If someone says something to me, I show them by scoring points.' Miller said. 'It pushes me harder when someone talks to me, but I don't need to do it. I let my play speak for itself.'"

Mark: That's cool that you got to see then what the rest of us saw later, the whole process of watching them blossom into stars but remaining true to who they were as kids.

André (smiling): Yes, I'm a proud papa.

Chris: This is good shit, Dré!

André: Oh, I'm not done!

I pulled out a July 16, 1995 issue.

André: I have a few more names for you. You guys ever heard of Corey Benjamin or Jason Hart?

Junior: Corey played for the Bulls at one time and Hart went to Syracuse.

André: "At the Nike Camp, Michael Bibby of Shadow Mountain High (Ariz.), son of former UCLA star Henry Bibby, starred for Best of the West along with Benjamin."

Junior: I loved Mike Bibby. That Sacramento (Kings) team he was on with Chris Webber should have won an NBA championship!

André: Well, this next name I'm going to give you is a reason why they didn't. Let's see if you've ever heard anything about him: "Two dozen Southland players competed in Sonny Vaccaro's Adidas/ABCD camp. The camp's best performer was 6-6 combo- guard Kobe Bryant, the son of former NBA star Joe (Jellybean) Bryant."

Chris: Holy shit!

Mark: KOBE!

Junior: You guys wrote about Kobe!?

André: Don't sleep on the *City Times*! We did our thing back in the day.

Chris: Damn! That *was* a dream job, huh? No wonder you were so depressed after all that shit went down!

André: Moving along.

Junior: I am *impressed*!

Mark: That makes three hall-of-famers your paper wrote about, along with Garnett and Pierce. Anybody else?

André: A couple of noteworthy names: Toby Bailey and Baron Davis. I watched both play in high school. Toby at Loyola before he went to UCLA in '94, and Baron at Crossroads (Santa Monica) before *he* went to UCLA in '97.

Mark: Didn't Toby win a national championship at UCLA?

André: Yup!

Chris: Any other names you wanna drop?

André: Well, we do have to get going for dinner. I don't want to hold us up any longer. I'm starving!

Junior: Me too!

André: But since Chris insisted, I did meet Oscar De La Hoya and Riddick Bowe up in Big Bear (California) while they were both training for upcoming fights.

Mark: For real?

André: Yup. Oscar was a cool guy. Very down to earth.

Mark: Oh, *Oscar* was … was he? Look at Mr. First-Name Basis over here!

André: Well you know what they say—"Those that can, do … those that can't, ask about it."

Chris (laughing): This fuckin' guy!

Junior: Uh-huh. *Okay*, did you actually *talk* to them?

André: Yeah, sort of. Oscar and I arrived at the buffet table at the same time. He had just finished sparring for two hours but told me to go ahead of him. He was very much a gentleman. That has always stuck with me. Riddick was taking questions from the reporters, so I just asked him something about his preparation for the fight. He answered me while impersonating Muhammad Ali—something he was known to do.

Mark: Very cool. I'm proud of you, brother. And very *impressed* as well!

André: Thanks, guys, that means a lot!

Chris: Do you ever miss it?

André: I wouldn't allow myself to miss it for a long time because it hurt too much! But after talking about Ice-T with Chris and reopening those old wounds, I think I am healing in a healthy way. Even sitting here talking with you guys helps me remember everything I enjoyed about writing and why I will always be a writer. I appreciate you guys for that!

Awkward silence.

Mark: I think someone just had a moment.

Junior: Definitely!

André: Nope.

Chris: I've had a few moments, and that is *definitely* what it looked and felt like.

André: All right, fine! Maybe a little one. My name is André, and I had a tiny moment.

Mark: There you go, own it!

Junior: Dinner, anyone?

André: Yeah, let's go!

Chris: So Dré, I have one more question …

André: Shoot.

Chris: What sticks out most in your mind: All of these awesome clippings or the one photo of our friend and his "sweet-swinging schlong?!"

Leave it up to Chris.

Mark: I say the schlong!

Junior: I second the schlong!

Chris: The schlong!

André: Moving along.

*All articles originally appeared in the *City Times* section of the *Los Angeles Times*. Sean Waters and Greg Hester contributed to some articles.

RETURN FLIGHT

There I sat in Shari's living room for the umpteenth time, discussing everything under the sun. In many ways, she had become my sounding board, the role I usually play for pretty much *everybody*—including her from time to time.

"Ginger has really taken a liking to you," she observed. "Look at how she just crawls up into your lap, curls up in a big fluffy white ball, and collapses! That's rare, because as you *know*—"

"Yes, Shari," I interrupted, "you are the only one she has really bonded with since you got her. I know!"

Ginger was the name given to the stray Shari had welcomed into her home. I didn't mind that she had bonded with me, because she was a beautiful cat! She had a sweet disposition and eyes so big and blue that if she were a he, Sinatra would be the obvious name of choice, after ole Blue Eyes himself.

Any time I left Shari's apartment, I always took a piece of Ginger with me—several pieces, actually. This cat could shed fur with the best of felines.

Shari wasn't surprised that I had cut her off mid sentence; we did that to each other all the time. What caught her attention was my rather terse response, to which she remarked, "*Well* ... somebody forgot to feed Mr. Grumpy today!"

"Very funny!"

"What's going on with you? ... Is something wrong?"

"No, nothing."

"Nothing as in nothing, or nothing as in something is, but I don't want to talk about it?"

"The first one."

"Meaning the second one! You should eat something—it will make you feel better."

I'm sure I should have been insulted on some level, but I found her cure-all to be a funny if not effective one. "So let me get this straight, Shari ... the answer as to how to improve a man's disposition is to feed him?"

"Hey, I didn't make the rules!" she pointed out. "You men are governed by your appetites, be it food or sex! Give a man one or the other—or both—and he will be easier to deal with."

"I'll try and remember that! Anyway, I ate before I came over."

"Must be sexual frustration, then."

I glared at Shari. She smirked back. "What's buggin' you, then?"

"Is this woman's intuition at work?"

"Nothing intuitive at all. You wrinkle your forehead whenever you are deep in thought or something is bothering you. Dead giveaway."

"And here I was, thinking you were highly perceptive!"

"And here I was, thinking you were a highly evolved member of your species who was beyond hiding his feelings when something was obviously bothering him!"

"Ouch!" I cried, shaking my hand as if it had been slapped. "Must you gender-bash at every turn?"

"Honey, I can't help it! You men provide so much material."

"You certainly know how to make a guy feel better."

"Dré, you know I *luvs* you!"

"What I know is based on your fondness of men—or lack thereof—some guy must have really done a number on you!"

Shari folded her legs and sat back against the couch. Holding her coffee mug with both hands, she slowly raised it to her lips before taking a long sip. Her head down, she raised only her eyes to look at me. "Who says it was a guy?"

"Well that makes sense, actually, because only a woman could make a person that bitter!"

Shari spit out some of her coffee while trying to keep from laughing. "Damn it, Dré!"

"Uh-huh. You know it's true!"

"Is not!"

"Really? Well then why did you just spray cappuccino all over your pajama pants?"

"Because you're stupid!"

Tapping my temple with my finger, I said, "Like a fox."

"Like an idiot! Now I have to go change my pants. While I'm gone, you think about what's going on with you, mister! And I want an honest answer when I get back." With that, Shari turned and walked toward her bedroom.

Rolling my eyes, I yelled, "Yes, ma'am."

She shouted back, "And don't you roll your *eyes* at me!"

As much as I hated to admit it, Shari was right. Something was going on with me, because I was off my game. There was a definite disturbance in the Force, but I wasn't about to admit that to the resident Yoda, so I tried to figure it out for myself like a good Jedi. Thinking back to when I had first started to feel this way, I narrowed it down to sometime during my drive back from Los Angeles last week.

Mallory had moved to Los Angeles from the East Coast earlier this year. She had gotten in touch with me about four months later, asking me to come visit. I did, and the next thing I knew, we had rekindled our once-torrid lust affair. Over the next eight weeks, I had a weekend girl to visit to fulfill all my sexual desires. Neither of us was looking for a relationship—*especially* with one another.

It was the perfect no-strings-attached situation, but something had happened along the way. The more I would hear her talk about these other guys she dated in the way she used to talk about me, I started to feel something. *Jealousy?* No, definitely not that! I wanted no part of a relationship with this woman.

What was it, then?

At some point, I had been overcome with unfamiliar feelings. They prompted me to think, *I'm good enough to have sex with this person whenever she feels the need, but I'm not good enough to be her partner?* (Yeah, she could make the same claim; but we'll wait for her book!) Could it be that I wanted to be seen as more than just a great lay, as she described me to her friends? Talk about an inopportune time to grow a pair of ovaries—I was about to ruin a great thing by breaking the cardinal rule of unattached random sex: Keep emotions out!

I was enjoying all the boyfriend privileges without all the boyfriend responsibilities: a few weekly phone calls for sex- preservation purposes, and that's it! A low-maintenance relationship with a high-maintenance woman. What a deal! And yet it still wasn't enough. Evolution sucks!

"By that dumb look on your face, Dré, I take it we're no closer to the truth?" Shari mocked me again. She reentered the room dressed in only a XXL tee shirt and booties, missing an obvious article of clothing.

"Um, Shari, I think you forgot your bottoms." Wait, I am telling an attractive half-naked woman to go put her pants on ... this problem is more serious than I thought!

"I have a thong on, Dré! Besides, it's just you, silly. You're always a gentleman, which is one of the things that I like about you."

I'd take that. "Thank you, Shari! I still haven't really figured out anything, though. I'm shooting blanks."

"Do yourself a favor and never repeat those words aloud at your job!" Shari cautioned. "That's how rumors get started."

"Funny, you are."

"We're doing *Star Wars* impersonations now?"

"The Force, I do need. Very disturbing, this problem is!"

Shari giggled. "Don't you start!" She had gone to the kitchen and prepared herself another cup of coffee while my mind was driving between the 405 and 805 freeways. "You want me to spit this out again?"

"No. Those naked legs, you will burn!"

Shari managed not to spit this time, but she couldn't avoid drooling some of the liquid down her cheek and chin in attempts to hold in her laughter. I put no such restraints on myself, however. "Funny, that was! Much better, I feel!"

"I'm glad," Shari grunted, wiping the spittle off her chin. "Good to know that you feel better at my expense."

"How does it feel?"

Shari rolled her eyes and mumbled, "Touché."

I touched the side of my mouth with a finger. "You missed a spot right …"

For my attempted assistance, I received the death stare. The Force is strong in this one.

Quickly switching gears, I acknowledged, "So, I, uh, really can't put my finger on it, but you are right. There has definitely been a weird energy going on around me lately."

"You know, Dré, you are a very intuitive person. I've noticed over the years how perceptive and sensitive you are to energy. You are definitely more in touch with your feminine side than most men I know!"

"Please, do *me* a favor," I pleaded. "Never repeat *those* words aloud at my job!"

"Ha-ha! I can see how they could be taken out of context."

"Mm-hm."

"Seriously, Dré, you are one of the sweetest guys I have ever met."

"Yeah, I am a sweetheart, aren't I?"

"Modest, too!"

"Overrated quality."

"I mean, you have a deep respect for women. I have learned that for myself. How about that time you told me you saw that one customer in the grocery store, shopping with his wife?"

I thought back. "You mean the guy who used to leave his underage son in the car while he came in the store right quick to get his jollies?" I snarled. "What about the jerk?"

"You could have basically ended his marriage right there if you had approached them, but you chose not to because, I'm sure, you were thinking about his wife and kid."

"They are *all* I was thinking about."

"See."

"But I can't lie! I did for a moment think about going over to them and saying something like 'Hello, ma'am. I see your husband prefers cream-style corn to whole-kernel, but I'm sure you know that already. Here's something you probably don't know: He prefers hand jobs from trannies, not heteros!'"

Shari burst into tears, laughing. As I waited for her to regain composure, I continued to gently run my fingers through Ginger's soft fur, starting at her head, each long stroke producing a fistful of fur by tail's end. She purred in delight.

"Oh my God, that was too funny!" Shari shouted. "Speaking of work, has anything changed that would be a cause of concern, perhaps?"

"Hmm, nothing I can think of. I mean, Sal did mention something the other day about store changes and possible closures, but that won't affect my situation."

"You know, maybe it's time for you to move on and do something different. You've been doing this job for nearly ten years. Maybe you're just burnt out."

Maybe she was right. Maybe deep down, I knew it was time for me to take that next step— whatever that was. Maybe I was going through some sort of internal struggle while coming to grips with this fact. Like it or not, if it was time to go, it wouldn't be easy for me to leave. I never could have imagined having this sentiment about a pornography shop. Likewise, I never could have dreamed an adult store could double as a social hub for entertainment, enlightenment, and education. Politics. Law. Religion. World Affairs. Sports. And of course, sex. No topic was off-limits. No profession was left off the guest list: doctor, lawyer, teacher, housewife, police officer, car dealer, gourmet chef. Even a missionary.

Just as I had given the inside of the store a facelift many times over, so had the shop allowed me to do some internal restructuring: rearranging priorities, reanalyzing beliefs, reassessing my value system. I had developed very special bonds with some very remarkable individuals, straight and gay, black and white—and all shades in between—rich and poor, religious and secular, addicts, the homeless, a nymphomaniac, a dominatrix.

An amazing journey.

It's ironic how a place that specializes in sex taught me about so many things that aren't related to sex at all: life lessons on belonging and acceptance, safety and security, guilt and shame—and the biggest of them all: *hypocrisy!* The store showed me how society both overvalues and undervalues the role of sex in a healthy relationship, how we misplace the emphasis on the *who*, *where*, *when*, and *how* we should have sex instead of focusing on the why. How we like to assign labels to a person or thing because it helps us to better cope with our own issues and insecurities about that person or subject. How what's really important is not where you work or who you work with, but what you take from the experience.

For nearly a decade, and for better or (sometimes) worse, my marriage to Video Expo changed my life in ways I never could have expected. The store had become one of my great loves, and part of me wasn't ready for the impending divorce (the second of my professional career).

"Earth to Dré!" Shari called out. "You suddenly got really quiet. Where did you go?"

I gathered my thoughts. "Nowhere," I responded. "But somewhere soon."

"Umm, *okay* ... you care to elaborate?"

"Not really. Just know that you have been a great friend to me and I appreciate you very much. Thank you!"

Shari beamed with pride. Taking in the compliment, she placed a hand over her heart. "Mutual, the feeling is … very welcome, you are!"

It had been about two weeks since I'd visited with Shari, but our conversation was still fresh in my mind—and, of course, some of Ginger's hair was still on my jacket. The feelings I was having about leaving intensified as talk regarding upcoming changes in the company continued to escalate.

I was now at the center of the scuttlebutt, sitting in the back of the main office while awaiting a product presentation by one of the store's major suppliers. Whispers of gossip circulated around the room: *What stores are closing? Who is getting laid off? When will it all happen?*

My mind was clear for a little while. The meeting (or perhaps the cleavage on the busty representative) proved to be an effective momentary distraction. Whichever the case, it was the first time in weeks that my mind was at ease.

Temporarily, anyway.

Bill, the owner of the company, whom I had gotten to know rather well over the years, tapped me on the shoulder and motioned for me to come to his office. I nodded and then abruptly turned back around, hoping not to attract attention to our not-so-private exchange.

Too late.

Eyes that had just been looking eagerly at top-of-the-line vibrators now gazed curiously in my direction, and there I was, left holding the bag, literally, after being interrupted by Bill. I had forgotten to continue to pass around the new bargain bundle (which included lube, condoms, and a free mini vibe) that the company was offering to first-time customers.

"Okay, whoever can give me the correct answers to this two-part question will get to take home a bargain bundle for free," the female rep said.

Whew! Unwanted attention diverted. Saved by the blonde.

"Vibrators were created to cure what medical condition?" she asked.

Aw … c'mon, guys! This is an easy one! Well, easy to anyone who watched that television special.

I knew the answer, but I certainly was not about to raise my hand. I did, however, quickly pass along the bargain bundle to the clerk sitting next to me.

A coworker finally spoke up. "I believe it was made to treat hysteria?" he guessed.

"Correct! Now, can you tell me *when* this happened?"

My coworker struggled to find the follow-up answer. "Um, I saw it on this show once, but I can't remember the time."

I stared at the blank faces in the room and knew no answer was forthcoming. I thought, *Ah, what the hell? I gotta make an exit anyway. It might as well be a grand one!* I piped up. "Nineteenth century: late 1800s, to be exact!"

"That's right, sir! You guys are very well informed."

And you, sweetheart, are very well endowed! No brain surgeon needed to figure out why you're here pitching to a mostly male audience.

And although I would love to sit here and continue to admire your plastic surgeon's work, this is my cue to exit stage left.

It was time to see the owner! I slowly approached the door to his office. Three polite knocks were greeted with "Come in!"

Once inside, I didn't see any plastic covering the furniture or floor—Yes, I watch a lot of mob movies!—a good thing. Bill gestured for me to sit in the chair across from him. I did. We were separated by a large mahogany desk with beautiful hand-carved designs. It probably cost a small fortune. (Peanuts to him, six months in rent to me.)

As Bill swiveled in his chair to turn away from his computer, a creaking noise sliced through the air—and the tension. Nervously, "Sounds like a job for WD-40," I joked.

He plopped a handful of papers onto the desk and scratched the back of his head. "Eh, I'll just get a new fuckin' chair!"

This was Bill's usual modus operandi: If something isn't working properly or satisfactorily, the solution is to not waste time or money trying to fix it—simply replace it! Employees were not excluded from his unwritten policy, either. Although Bill was a bit more lenient with his workers, poor work performance or unreliability on their part would quickly lead to scheduling changes, lesser hours, and, eventually, termination. During my time at the company, I had been written up only twice: once for playing blackjack with coworkers, and the other for doodling sketches at the counter—babysitting grown men can get boring after a while—but I had never received a write-up for being incompetent or a no-call/no-show. This added to my confusion about why Bill had called me into his office.

"Well ... sales have been down in several of our stores," Bill began.

Shit.

"Including yours." Holy shit!

"You have been a great employee during your time here!"

Famous fuckin' last words.

"I haven't talked to anyone else yet, but I was thinking ... it might be time for a change."

Wow! So I'm first to get the guillotine, eh?! You're going to use me to sharpen the blade for everyone else? After all I've done for this company?!

Bill continued, "When you became manager at Video Expo, you really cleaned up the store and made it profitable again."

That's right! So, Robespierre, why, now that it's time for your little revolution, are you treating me like the enemy and sending me to the gallows? Was this what had been bothering me all along? Had my feelings really been a premonition about my second execution at the work-place? At a porn store, no less?! Talk about adding insult to injury! Don't get me wrong— as I've stated before, my time at the shop had proven invaluable to my growth as an individual, but seriously, who gets fired from a porn shop?!

Bill slowly leaned back in his chair, which squealed even louder with the shift in weight. He held a pen in his left hand and placed the eraser at the corner of his mouth. "I can't thank you enough for what you have done for my business!"

Odd way to thank somebody! Feels less like a thank-you and more like a fuck-you!

"That's why, André, I'm going to show you my appreciation!"

I waited, confused.

"The time has come to turn Video Expo into a discount store! I'm taking a financial hit because customers aren't buying the higher-priced items. The clientele at your store like to bargain shop, so we will flood it with lower-priced merchandise and advertise accordingly."

Pretty sure someone suggested doing this before.

"You mentioned a while back that I should consider doing something like this, so I took it into consideration. From that point on, I started focusing on what was really selling at that location and noticed your recommendation was a good one."

"Thank you, Bill!" I answered, my first words in nearly two minutes. Apparently, I had escaped the beheading, but my fate was still unclear to me. "I'm still confused as to where I fit into all this."

"Well, I'm closing down a few locations because they just aren't making enough money, but I bought out some properties and I am going to open up new stores."

"Really?"

"Yes."

"Where?"

"One in Washington. Two in Ohio. One in Miami—near South Beach."

"South Beach?!"

"Yeah, I was thinking about asking you if you would be interested in relocating out there, but I thought it better to send someone who is fluent in Spanish."

Fuck! I *knew* I should have used that Rosetta Stone software and learned Spanish two years before when I had the chance. *Fuck me!*

"However ..." Bill hesitated before finishing, "I think I found the perfect place for you."

More perfect than South Beach? Are you kidding me?!

"Well, I just bought a large space in a prime money-making location," Bill bragged. "Near two major freeways. Our product is in high demand there. It's an area where the median age is about thirty- six years old. Just perfect."

That's when I started to hear it again. It had been almost ten long years since I had last heard that sound. But it was back!

"Is something wrong?" Bill asked. "You seem preoccupied."

"No, it's nothing," I pretended. "Thought I heard something. Please continue. So, where is this porn utopia?" Wait a minute ... *Porn Utopia?* Product in high demand. Major free-ways. 'Just perfect!' Is he talking about ...?

Bill smiled at me from across his desk and folded his arms. "It's a place you are quite familiar with, André. It's your old stomping grounds—the Valley!"

At that point, the entire office seemed to echo with laughter! Oddly enough, it didn't bother me—probably because, unlike last time, I didn't feel like the joke was on me. It was almost as if I was being invited to join in on the hilarity. I then realized I had come full circle. It was time to go back. Time to show my ex how much I had matured. Time to show her the man I had become. To reveal the lessons I had learned.

I looked up and smiled at Bill. "Los Angeles, huh?"

"Yes, sir! Los Angeles."

What Bill didn't know was that I had a surprise or two for him. Life, indeed, is all about timing! "You know, Bill, I've been working on this book."

"Oh?"

"Yes! It's about the unique experiences that take place in your stores, involving the one-of-a-kind patrons and their intriguing stories."

"Hmm," he pondered.

"You know," I continued, "no other store owners have a book memorializing their outfit and its day-to-day operations—which will also be brought to light by the occupational reality show, by the way."

"The what?! Reality show? What reality show?"

"Oh yeah! If people love *Pawn Stars* and *Duck Dynasty*, imagine if we gave them a look inside one of the most controversial, taboo, and profitable businesses there is! And can you imagine how much the companies will pay to have their products shown on a hit television show?"

As visions of dollar signs danced in Bill's head, I continued to reel him in. "Of course, they'll all take a backseat to your new Fantasyland Luxury line."

"My what?"

"*Your* product line. Just like Albertson's and Walgreens have their own line of products, so should you! That will be a part of your branding. Everyone will know about the man with thirty adult establishments across the country. I've heard you consider yourself the Walmart of porn.

It's time to show the world! Of course, the cable show will definitely help out with that!"

"Cable show?!"

"Yeah. I've been working on a script that's loosely based off the book. I've talked to a few people in and out of the industry about it ... shared some of the ideas and concepts with them—and they believe it's a 'hit in waiting'!"

"Wait, wait, hold on a second," Bill stopped me. "You're working on a book. Reality show. Product line. Cable show ..."

"Well, the book is finished," I interjected. "The pilot for the cable show is done. The other things are all dependent upon you. I didn't even mention the publishing company, Pen The Tale Publishing, that I've started. I already have three people lined up who are working on books as we speak."

"Like yours?"

"No. One is a book of poems. One is a book of photographs taken by a friend I knew at the *City Times*, who has worked at the LA Times for nearly twenty-five years. Another is a book outlining skills and strategies for reducing conflicts and building solid connections between parents and children. I have some solid investment opportunities for you. Sound business ventures."

Amazed, Bill asked, "You came up with all this on your own?"

"Well, it started a few years ago with me writing the book. Shortly thereafter, I stared putting a plan together with Jacques—you know, the janitor over at my store?"

"Right."

"When he found out what I was doing, I found out he had a head for business, and the rest is, as they say, *history!*"

Still taking everything in, Bill, who had been standing up, sat back down in his chair, shaking his head. He started to speak a few times but stopped himself each time out of bewilderment.

I helped him out. "Considering everything I just told you, it looks like Los Angeles would be the ideal place for me, huh?"

"Does that mean ..."

"Yes, count me in! *Us*, actually. I'd like Jacques to join me, if possible—him being my business partner, and all."

"I think we can work something out."

"Great! How about we set up a meeting so we can come in and present the entire package to you?"

"Excellent!"

With a gentleman's shake, it was done. I was to come in the following day to discuss the particulars and to set a time and date for our presentation.

As I walked outside to my car, I noticed the parking lot was littered with customers making their way into the store. "Gee, you're in a good mood!" one of them said to me in passing. "You're smiling from ear to ear."

I *was* in a good mood! I was in a good place. Because this time around, I was laughing, too!

A very special thank you to Steve Wiener for all his support during the book-writing process, and whose stores helped provide the inspiration for these stories.

The following is a list of his store locations nationwide:

Adult Pleasures #01, 4404 N. Detroit Ave. Toledo, OH 43613

Adult Pleasures #02, 5365 Monroe St. Toledo, OH 43623

Cahuenga Video, 1651 North Cahuenga Blvd. Hollywood, CA 90028

Eastside Arcade, 863 Valley Mall Pkwy. East Wenatchee, WA 98802

Fantasyland, 1157 Sweetwater Rd. Spring Valley, CA 91977

Fantasyland #02, 16016 SE 82nd Dr. Clackamas, OR 97015

Intimates & Adult Superstore, 203 North Houston Ln. Lodi, CA 95240

L'Amour Shoppe #01, 323 E. Alisal St. Salinas, CA 93901

L'Amour Shoppe #02, 2329 El Camino Real St. Santa Clara, CA 95050

L'Amour Shoppe #03, 40555 B Grimmer Blvd. Fremont, CA 94538

L'Amour Shoppe #04, 22553 Main St. Hayward, CA 94541

L'Amour Shoppe #06, 1507 B 9th St. Modesto, CA 95354

L'Amour Shoppe #07, 2531 Broadway. Sacramento, CA 95818

Mercury Books #01, 8081 Balboa Ave. San Diego, CA 92111

Mercury Books #02, 7435 Clairmont Mesa Blvd. San Diego, CA 92111

Perez Images, 68366 Perez Rd. Cathedral City, CA 92234

Quail Roost Adult Video, 10348 SW 186th St. Miami, FL 33157

Venus Faire, 6452 Lankershim Blvd. North Hollywood, CA 91606

Video Exchange, 7656 Broadway Ave. San Diego, CA 91945

X-Spot #02, 1901 South Alameda Blvd. Los Angeles, CA 90058

X-Spot #04, 6586 E. Washington Blvd. Commerce, CA 90040

X-Spot #05, 3537 West Sunshine St. Springfield, MO 65807

X-Spot #09, 3606 Midway Dr. San Diego, CA 92110

X-Spot #10 1111 N 1st St. #5, Yakima, WA 98901

Yakima Arcade, 27 South Front St. Yakima, WA 98901

Zebulon Enterprises, 24 West 777 Lake St. Roselle, IL 60172

Printed by Libri Plureos GmbH in Hamburg, Germany